"*Party of One* covers all the bases with convincingly argued ways to change your POV. Myth-busters Meghan Keane and LA Johnson have created an illustrated guidebook to one of life's most important things, loving your own company. Their grounded research is delivered with a touch of humor and dose of personal experience."

WHITNEY SHERMAN, illustrator and educator

"Where was this book when I needed it? *Party of One* is a refreshing answer to the tired, clichéd notions of romantic love that keep many of us stuck and spinning in a loop of self-loathing. With humor, compassion, and candor, Keane takes readers on a quest to reexamine what we often take for granted about relationships, offering insights to cultivate a fulfilling relationship with the only person on earth who can offer us unconditional love—ourselves. Through introspection and self-inquiry, this book guides readers towards a deeper understanding of themselves and the deep fulfillment that comes only from journeying within."

BRITT FRANK, LSCSW, author of *The Science of Stuck* and *The Getting Unstuck Workbook*

"Who hasn't struggled at times with a nagging inner critic, the sting of rejection, or the pain of being alone? *Party of One* expertly explores these common experiences, pointing out how common they are on the one hand, while also providing readers with science-based strategies to help them skillfully manage them. Charmingly written and filled with actionable tools, this book provides readers with an essential roadmap for navigating their emotions."

ETHAN KROSS, international bestselling author of *Chatter*

PARTY OF
ONE

BE YOUR OWN
BEST LIFE PARTNER

MEGHAN KEANE
ART BY **LA JOHNSON**

CHRONICLE PRISM

Library of Congress Cataloging-in-Publication Data available.

ISBN 978-1-7972-2752-8

Manufactured in China.

Design by Pamela Geismar. Typeset in Freight Text, Neutra, and LA Johnson's ComicHands.

10 9 8 7 6 5 4 3 2 1

Chronicle books and gifts are available at special quantity discounts to corporations, professional associations, literacy programs, and other organizations. For details and discount information, please contact our premiums department at corporatesales@chroniclebooks.com or at 1-800-759-0190.

$\int_{0}^{1}$ CHRONICLE PRISM

Chronicle Prism is an imprint of Chronicle Books LLC
680 Second Street, San Francisco, California 94107

www.chronicleprism.com

CONTENTS

Introduction

THERE IS A HAZE. A CLOUDY, ALL-CONSUMING haze that can engulf a person. It's cotton-candy soft, so it doesn't feel like a threat. In fact, the haze is comforting; it tells you what you need to do. What you desire. When the haze whispers in your ear, you nod in agreement.

Yes! A partnership is what I want! Marriage is where my life is headed! A wedding is the coronation day for my adulthood. Let's go get it!

The haze approves.

The haze strokes your head when things feel bad. When dates go poorly, when you're spending a Friday night alone, when your heart aches at the sight of a couple kissing on the street—the haze tells you that you ought to feel bad. Don't you want what they have?

As years pass by, the haze hugs you tighter. But it's no longer a comfortable embrace. *Try harder! Go on more dates! Ask your aunt's friend's daughter who you've met a handful of times if they know someone because "you never know!"*

After a while, the haze doesn't feel helpful anymore. It feels claustrophobic. You pick at the haze, try to shoo it away. You don't even remember how it enveloped you in the first place—and yet it's come to dictate so many of your thoughts and feelings.

Worse, it's started to feel like others agree with your haze. Bewildered, they ask how it is that you're still single since you're just so great. Or can we set you up with a random colleague you have nothing in common with? Or worst of all, "*I don't know how you do it.*"

The haze tells you to listen to them. These people know what they are talking about, after all. They are coupled! Partnered! Married! They must know something you don't.

You sigh. But this is what you want, right? So you drag yourself to dates you don't want to go on. You keep your eyes open at every social function, scanning for potential mates. You spend endless hours swiping on what seems to be the same group of people you swiped left on yesterday.

It is exhausting and demoralizing.

What the haze doesn't want you to know, but what I'm here to tell you, is that there is a way out. You can poke your head out of this cloud—this unpleasant pressure built from culture and history and others' misplaced good intentions—and emerge under a clear sky.

● ● ●

I never thought I would have to work to find a partner. I never thought I'd read stacks of self-help books about dating. I simply assumed that when I became an adult, I would naturally find a partner without trying.

College came and went. *That's fine!* I thought. *I'm so young! Let's see what happens when I start working.* My early twenties slid into my late twenties—still not a serious partner in sight.

Then I found the promise of a boyfriend. I was twenty-six years old when we met. I felt insecure that I had never been in a "you're my boyfriend and I'm your girlfriend" relationship before, and I'm embarrassed to admit how much of a confidence boost that first relationship gave me. But it was an ugly kind of confidence. I felt smug holding his hand in public. I felt I had crossed the threshold into an exclusive club.

I was so blinded by my excitement of having coupled status that I missed obvious signs that the relationship was not going to work. We fought over insignificant things, like whether it's okay to spoil movies. I swept his complicated relationship with his father under the rug. When he casually said he didn't know if he wanted children as we walked past some kids running a sidewalk lemonade stand, I didn't ask any follow-up questions.

Don't mess this up, I thought. *It took you so long to get here.*

Six months later, I went on a family vacation to Italy. After a beautiful week of bingeing on pasta and stunning coastal views, I called my boyfriend on my drive home from the airport. It was immediately clear something was off. I made him spit it out. He told me that I was super wonderful—but he just didn't love me enough. After dumping me, he immediately found a long-term partner.

I had been stripped of my shiny coupled-up badge and sent packing. I emotionally crashed hard. I spent months ruminating over how this had happened and what it said about me. *I'm running behind. People think I'm pathetic, don't they? What is wrong with me?*

Another promising boyfriend came a year later. There was another swell of that ugly confidence. I hadn't learned my lesson yet, so no deep questions about values or life goals were broached. After telling me I was super wonderful, but he just didn't love me enough, this boyfriend also dumped me and immediately found a long-term partner.

I tried not to read this as a trend. And I tried to feel okay.

But all of a sudden, some kind of weird clock started ticking. It told me I was running out of time to partner up. Intellectually, I knew that love and partnership could come in all shapes and sizes (and at all ages), but that damn clock kept ticking. It was maddening. As I became depressed by my single status, I felt increasingly disgusted with myself that I even cared in the first place.

After a few dark years of depression, I knew something had to change. It felt like I had no power in my relationships, which meant I was always on uneven ground. I had had enough. I decided that the people I dated were no longer going to hold the keys to my happiness. I needed to be in control of my own self-worth. I needed to slam that ticking clock against the wall. To unzip myself from that haze once and for all and create a better reality for myself.

I started by coming up with a list of things I had the power to change. This list turned out to be very short:

1) myself. I needed to untangle myself from the lie that true happiness only exists in a romantic relationship. I needed to clear the clouds of expectation and dissatisfaction following me around, making my world feel endlessly gray. I needed to celebrate those things about me that were wonderful and forgive myself for those things that were perhaps a little less so. I needed to spend time with myself and give myself space to grow—while also preserving some space for community and connection with others. I needed to stop ruminating myself into a miserable state. I needed to stop being such a jerk to myself.

These were things I didn't have to wait for a partner to accomplish. In essence: I would treat myself with the same love I had eagerly sought to give others. I could be my own soulmate.

This book is not about how to date smarter or how to get yourself "ready" for a partner. Instead, this book is about nurturing the most important relationship you'll ever have—the one you have with yourself. You will learn how to shed the pressure to partner and empower yourself to cultivate your own inner validation. Love is not one-size-fits-all, and the overwhelming pressure to find one specific—often heterosexual and monogamous—type of love hurts everyone. It cuts us off from finding nourishing connections of all different kinds in our lives. This book rejects those constraints and aims to support you—and me and everyone—living life more fully.

Some other notes: I'm a straight white woman, so some of the pressures and norms I face don't apply to everyone.

My goal is to provide tools everyone can benefit from, but I know my experience is not universal. I should also note that this book is *not* anti-partnership. Nor is it anti-marriage (although I will get into some not-so-flattering facts about marriage shortly). I believe people are able to make their own choices about what, if any, kinds of partnership will best support them. Perhaps that means a monogamous marriage or an open one. Maybe it means co-parenting kids with a friend or another communal living arrangement. Or being partnered but never married. The choice about whether or how you partner is yours alone.

This is the book I wish I had had when I was trapped in my own haze, and while this book is primarily written for single people, it is my hope that it will help *anyone* see a way to a better future for themselves. Regardless of your relationship status, everyone is capable of feeling lonely or lost. Whether you're here because you feel stuck as a single person, because you are feeling lonely in a relationship, or because you are uncomfortable spending time with yourself, this book will hold your hand and show you a gentler path to building a life you love, no matter your relationship status.

So, what's ahead? First, we will dive into societal expectations and learn more about the history of marriage—and why it's not necessarily the ideal institution we all should strive toward. Then we are going to take some time to meet ourselves. We'll take emotional inventory and think through what we really need instead of what we think we do. Next, we'll go deep into our pesky (but trainable!) brains and explore tools for breaking harmful rumination loops. Then we're going to mentally map out our lives, independent of partnership. What kinds of dreams do we have and what are the values that we want our lives to embody? Next, we will learn how to sit with our emotions—the good and the bad— instead of treating them like enemies. And lastly, we'll talk about building community and learning how to appreciate the many forms it can take. At the end of each chapter there will be ideas for practices and activities to help reinforce the tools we've learned.

My hope is that you will not just have a shift in perspective but that you will really feel a change within you. This book is a resource to help you bridge the gap between knowing it is possible to feel secure and happy on your own and feeling that truth deep in your soul and body.

I can already see that haze disappearing now.

1

Demystifying Romantic Love and Marriage

IF YOU'RE SOMEONE WHO'S SINGLE AND hoping to be partnered eventually, pursuing partnership can feel like you're playing a cruel version of Chutes and Ladders. Your goal is to get to square one hundred, where your romantic partner is waiting for you. But because the game is all luck, you can slip down a long-ass slide at random. On your way down, you see other people climbing ladders. Your girlfriend who recently left a five-year relationship just met someone at work and now they are fully committed without seeming to break a sweat. Your brother keeps finding amazing woman after amazing woman. Your best guy friend met a wonderful guy at a bar and now they are on a fabulous vacation together. Meanwhile, you can barely have a conversation with a person from a dating app that doesn't make you want to pull out your own teeth.

The reality is that everyone is on their own timeline, but that doesn't make it feel any less unfair when you're sliding down that chute back to square one after a connection just didn't work out. Where does that feeling of "losing" even come from? Why do we even need to think of a romantic partner as something to "win"? These attitudes are reflected in the language we use when friends and family get partnered:

"Finally!"

"Congratulations!"

"It's about time!"

It can feel like people are really saying *Congrats on escaping singledom where you would have rotted away forever if you didn't finally find that escape hatch!*

Society tells us that partnered people are somehow more whole, satisfied, and accomplished, and that single people are therefore lacking. Personally, I think it's a tiny miracle when people happily partner. It represents a beautiful mix of timing, luck, and shared values. But it's not some kind of moral victory.

Instead of defaulting to the idea of partnership as the ultimate prize, it's time to reexamine the myths about our allegedly categorical need for romantic partnership. To start, let's talk about what many consider the pinnacle of partnership: marriage. While not everyone wants to get married, its cultural primacy shapes many different kinds of partnership in our society.

So many people are clamoring to be married (or, let's be honest, for some folks, salivating to have a wedding), but what does that even mean? Conceptions of marriage, of course, change within different contexts of culture, gender, sexuality, and more. But in our Western culture, the messaging of movies, fairy tales, and even the narratives spun by our own families and friends reinforce that haze of romantic expectations and disappointment. It's easy to slip into the thinking that being married is the correct way for an adult to live, and, further, that marriage somehow validates your worth as a human being.

I grew up during the Disney princess renaissance. There was the mermaid who gave up her voice to be with a man, the provincial French girl who fell in love with her captor, the princess with a cool pet tiger who was charmed by the man who lied about his identity. All these movies spend a lot of time talking (and singing!) about how beautiful the princess is and how much she loves her paramour. Amazing songs in all these movies, by the way. But not exactly glowing examples of women secure in their self-worth and just fine on their own. These narratives teach heterosexual boys that women need saving. From what? A life of singleness. It also glamorizes men being the sole provider in a partnership. And LGBTQ+ narratives (with the exception of queer-coded villains) are left out of these fairy tales almost completely.

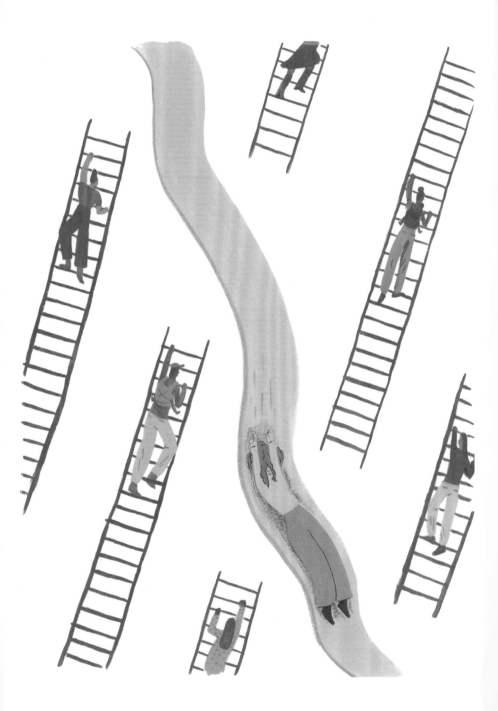

Fairy tales might also be responsible for our cultural obsession with weddings. Fairy tales were originally fables meant to teach lessons about what to wish for in life and the proper way to get it. Ruth Bottigheimer, a fairy-tale expert at Stony Brook University, says fairy tales embody aspiration and hope. Let's imagine you're back in the seventeenth century and, outside of religious texts, folk and fairy tales are really the only stories available. You hear the one about a peasant girl who marries up into royalty and gets a fancy wedding. You might think, *That sounds amazing; Cinderella is killing it.* You, too, might aspire to be a woman who gets rewarded with a prince and a white wedding gown for being "good."

Everyone knows the princess problem and how fairy tales play a role in the widespread obsession over marriage—plenty of scholarly exploration down that path—but I know from my own experience that they're not quite the whole story. By the time I got to middle school, I knew I didn't actually want to be a princess. Or at least I knew the limitations of those myths and archetypes. But it was impossible not to pick up on all the ways people in my life talked about the idea of partnership as some kind of final destination. Adults would often say the phrase "One day when you're married . . ." to me as a child. Leaning against our lockers, waiting for class, my girlfriends and I would speculate about which of us would get married first. There was always gossip about high school classmates who were dating. Even the most awkward teenage couples seemed so adult to me.

The closer you were to adulthood, the closer you were to checking off these coveted life milestones. Looking back on it, this urgency makes no sense to me. Why rush? If I race to check everything off, to reach the "finish line," then what? Did I think that once I got the partner, the kids, the house, all the things I'd been conditioned to want, that I could bask in the perfect glow of my so-called achievements and nothing bad would ever happen to me ever again? We know, logically, that's not how it works. Married people experience loss, pain, and struggles, too. So why be so singularly focused on getting to that destination?

Yet like so many of us, I was still seduced by the promise of romantic love. My steady diet of teen rom-coms and dramas like *She's All That*, *A Walk to Remember*, *The Prince and Me*, and other cringey late '90s and 2000s movies, where a beautiful young woman is treated like an ogre simply because she wears glasses and a ponytail, made me feel like landing the elusive boyfriend would complete me. I felt like romantic love would somehow elevate my worth, that my life couldn't really begin until I had a person who'd picked me by my side.

Side note: This is not to disparage all rom-coms. At their best, a romantic comedy can show that at the core of a good romantic relationship is real friendship (looking at you *When Harry Met Sally*). But most rom-coms end when the couple gets together—before the fights about the finer points of their budget or the difficult conversations about whether they should have kids. Here's where I give special mention to *My Best Friend's Wedding*—a movie in which Julia Roberts and her perfect curls jump through ever-more embarrassing hoops to break up her friend and his fiancée so she doesn't "end up alone." Her desperation is driven by what we've all been told about single women: that they are lonely and pitiable. I don't admire her quest, but I do love how by the end of the movie she's dancing with another friend. She is not alone; there has been love by her side the whole time.

For my money, it was these pop-culture stereotypes of single women, in particular, that largely drove my hunger for romantic love. Everything I watched and read and listened to was telling me that to be without a boyfriend meant social isolation. It meant being a freak, a loser. Now that I'm older, I see how all the qualities that I now love about myself—my outspokenness, my sense of humor, my nerdy interests—were the ones my culture was telling me I needed to suppress in order to find my Freddie Prinze Jr. But the messaging in the early 2000s went even further. The particularly gross-out teen sex comedies of the time told me that everything about me was all wrong—I didn't just need a boyfriend, I needed to be rail thin for my low-rise jeans, my curly hair pin straight, my attitude ever so "chill." The seemingly lighthearted entertainment of my childhood had morphed into a high school bully telling me I simply wasn't good enough on every level. These bad feelings were compounded by the rise of dating apps. Each time I was ghosted or a guy picked someone else over me after a few dates, the message felt cumulative. I'm not good enough.

If your "worth" is what is allegedly at stake, of course being single might make you feel in a dire state. But this hyperfocus on some future end goal puts us in danger of missing out on what's happening around us right now. I don't

want to devalue the life I have because I am waiting around for some future that's not guaranteed, nor guaranteed to be great. Marriage can be wonderful and meaningful. But because it involves humans, it is flawed just like we are. Settling for the wrong person just so you can be married is, in my opinion, a fate perhaps worse than death. Happiness is not a destination and neither is partnership.

Maybe marriage is something you truly want in life. That is totally fair. There are plenty of positive examples of how marriage and partnership can look. But it's important to stay grounded in reality. So let's unplug from the marriage matrix and take a quick tour through the supposedly hallowed halls of matrimony.

Myth #1: Marriage has always been for love.

Sure, we know there have been plenty of marriages throughout human history that were born of romantic love. But, historically, love has never been the primary reason for marriage. There's debate about how exactly marriage came to be and about its original core tenets. Some scholars say it was, flat-out, a means to oppress women. Others contend it was supposed to protect women (although that feels like a big stretch!). Others believe it arose out of evolutionary gender roles—based on the essentialist theory that men are hunters and women are gatherers, so their pairing up just "makes sense" (more on that myth later).

While the particulars differ, what does seem to be proven is that throughout history, marriage has been a tool for the transfer of power and property. Marriage helped grease the wheels for alliances among families. It didn't hurt that a union could also lead to a nice windfall. In her book *Marriage, a History: How Love Conquered Marriage,* historian Stephanie Coontz writes that before banks and the free market, marriage was the primary institution that allowed people to expand their resources and influence. For those living in a lower class, marriage could result in gaining a little extra property, and more labor, including potential children, for the family business. One grim example of this utilitarian approach to marriage is found in early eighteenth-century Marseille, France, when a marriage boom closely followed a deadly plague. These new marriages weren't exactly due to plague survivors suddenly overcome with a renewed sense of joie de vivre after a trauma, Coontz writes. No. It was that lots of people had died and there was land up for grabs. A quick way to acquire that freed-up land? Marry into it.

"Underneath that image [of traditional marriage] was a much more complex reality."

— Stephanie Coontz

For upper-class people, marriage has historically been an important tool in the politics of power. In fourteenth-century

Mexico, Azcapotzalco ruler Tezozomoc practiced something called interdynastic hypogamy, which is when a ruler marries off a daughter to a less powerful family in their kingdom. This is a particularly helpful practice when the ruler is looking to secure loyalty among lower-status subjects. Coontz writes about one eighteenth-century BCE ruler of Mari (current-day Syria), King Zimri-lim. This king married off eight of his daughters to rulers of vassal cities in a territory he had newly taken over. She writes, too, of a practice in ancient Egypt of "marriages" between humans and gods as a means to consolidate power. One Egyptian pharaoh in the eighth century BCE inducted his daughter into the divine wife club by "marrying" her to the god Amun and installing her as a puppet ruler in the strategically valuable region of Thebes—a marriage of convenience to help manage his far-away estates.

Even if many marriages today are not the result of scheming royalty, policy and law is baked into the institution. Up until 1979, head and master laws in the United States gave husbands the final say over property and household decisions without their wives' consent or knowledge necessary. Women couldn't have their own credit cards until the 1970s, when the Equal Credit Opportunity Act was enacted. Marital rape was not a crime in every state until 1993. These examples are all relatively recent in US history. So the next time you're romanticizing that fairy-tale union, it's important to remember that, in reality, the bonds of marriage have been used as tools for money, power, and, at times, oppression. Not exactly the kinds of things you toast at a wedding reception.

Myth #2: A heterosexual marriage with the man as provider and the woman as homemaker is the natural order of things!

Let's talk about prehistoric humans. I know looking to early humans to understand how the modern world operates can be a deeply flawed cliché. But the stories we tell ourselves are powerful—and it turns out we've been telling a tall tale about our prehistoric ancestors.

Think of an old-school diorama at a natural history museum: a dramatic tableau depicting the life of an early man—a lone hunter contending with a large predator to support his family. Back at the cave, a woman is tending the fire, minding the children, and collecting nuts and seeds.

Because we're myth-busting here, you already know where this is going. This image of early humans is not accurate, or not fully. There's evidence that the lone hunter was not all that common in early human tribes. Which makes a lot of sense when you think about what it would take to kill a large animal with few or no weapons. Are we to believe that these brave men were straight-up strangling lions and other scary carnivores with their bare hands without fail? In truth, hunting game was more of a group effort—likely undertaken with the help of nets, traps, and snares—and the group often included women and children. On these hunts, women and children would gather insects, fruit, nuts, and plants, too.

Agriculture hadn't been developed yet, meaning tribes often had to move around to find the resources to survive. Communities weren't made up of nuclear families with 2.5 kids living in independent caves. Early humans moved in large groups, often sharing food among the whole tribe. Because of this sharing economy, a woman didn't really need to be tied to one male provider to have enough to eat.

Also countering the notion of the caveman suburbia lifestyle is evidence of polyamory. While there's dispute about exactly how common polyamory was, we do know it occurred. Some scholars argue that polyamory was a way to strengthen social cohesion. Others say it was a result of a more egalitarian culture. For me, I am less interested in knowing if humans were always monogamous or always polyamorous than I am comforted to know there has always been some kind of variation in how life can be, including a more cooperative society with gender-flexible roles.

Myth #3: Marriage for romantic love has been around for a long time.

In the Western world, love as the central reason for getting hitched really didn't take hold until the nineteenth century. What accounts for its rise during this time? Pop culture strikes again. Much of the popular literature of the time—think *Jane Eyre*—romanticized the idea of marrying for love. *Pride and Prejudice* was a massive hit in the Regency era, long before the hand flex moment of the 2005 film. The story of Elizabeth Bennet, a woman who puts pursuing the romantic love of an intellectual equal above a practical marriage that would save her family from financial ruin, was so popular that its first edition entirely sold out—and it's still in print more than two hundred years later.

There was also a shift during the Victorian era from an emphasis on community to that of the private home. The idea of prioritizing your private family life began to be seen as more moral. During this time in America, there was also a shift from larger, public gatherings to more private affairs when celebrating holidays. This idea of the primacy of the immediate family and the domestic home, at least to me, feels like the seeds of modern marriage anxiety. An unmarried person doesn't just miss out on the potential of shared property; they will also be left out in the cold, literally, while other families celebrate holidays together all warm and cozy inside.

Perhaps a sneakier force at play is capitalism. Following the Industrial Revolution, wage labor jobs became more prevalent than work on family farms. This meant people were less reliant on their immediate families for survival—it was more possible to go off and start an independent life. According to Coontz, these new economic conditions combined with popular Enlightenment ideas of individualism and personal happiness laid the groundwork for a big change. When there was less of a necessity to marry for economic survival, what was supposed to motivate people to join in marriage? Love. Ah, the birth of "you complete me" but with petticoats.

But even if you were freer to pursue a love match, choosing a partner was a scary notion at the time, Coontz told me. There were cases of what was called "marriage trauma," where Victorian women became consumed with worry that they would marry the wrong man. And, to be clear, the ideal of Victorian marriage isn't a partnership dedicated to equality. In her book, *Courtship and Marriage in Victorian England*, Professor Jennifer Phegley, who specializes in transatlantic nineteenth-century literature, writes, "These high expectations focused on creating a home life that was a fortress

against the corrupting forces of the outside world." Phegley notes that Victorian marriages had a strong emphasis on "mutual loyalty, duty and protection," which at the time meant a woman submitting to her husband as the virtuous "angel in the house" who was responsible for the moral uprightness of her husband and home.

In modern times it's easy to think of love as always being the essential prerequisite for marriage or partnership. We certainly put a massive amount of expectation on that key factor. But for me, it's clarifying to know that marrying for love wasn't always a given and that the supremacy of romantic love is not wholly pure, eternal, or unchanging. Humans and our institutions are always bumping up against the circumstances of money, culture, and societal standards. Let's not pretend romantic love was always a given.

Myth #4: The best marriage is a "traditional marriage."

"Traditional marriage" is an interesting phrase. Traditional to who, exactly?

In Western culture, traditional marriage tends to imply a monogamous, heterosexual marriage with a strong emphasis on the patriarch in power. In politics, the idea of a traditional marriage is often used as a weapon against gay marriage rights and to discriminate against anyone trying to live and love outside of its narrow definition. It also historically has undertones of white supremacy—in the early twentieth century, American eugenicists sought to promote "traditional" marriages between white upper-class people with harmful propaganda disguised as relationship self-help books. At its core, the "traditional marriage" myth is exclusionary, homophobic, and racist.

Let's go beyond those basic facts. Think about all the ways that modern culture talks about marriage: It's a big deal! The biggest decision you'll ever make in your life! It's going to be the person you're with forever, so make sure you've found The One! But as we've already seen, scratch the surface of the history and you'll find that those attitudes about marriage have always been in flux.

Let's fast-forward to the 1950s in America—an era that tends to be thought of as the pinnacle of so-called traditional marriage. This was purportedly a time in American history when you would meet your soulmate in high school and live out a very specific dream of squeaky clean, domestic paradise in the suburbs—a cultural memory of marriage as an ideal *Leave It to Beaver*-style family unit. A man was the sole earner, the wife was the homemaker, and the two dutiful kids played happily in the yard with, say it with me, the white picket fence.

When people talk about traditional marriage now, it's a bit of a composite. It blends ideas of the male breadwinner at the center of the family and a woman spending lots of time with her kids while tending the home, and adds a dash of "simpler times" (often dog-whistling toward a pre–civil rights movement America). Traditional marriage to some suggests a time when the pressures of modern life were nonexistent. "They all get mixed up in people's minds because none of those things were traditional," historian Coontz told me. "As it turns out, of course, underneath that image was a much more complex reality."

After World War II there was an extraordinary spike in marriages. Women in the 1950s generally got married at a much younger age than even sixty years prior. Around 1890, the median age of an American woman at her first marriage was twenty-two years old. That dropped to a median age of 20 by 1950. A two-year difference might not sound all that impressive, but it seems to be the last time in American history that this number dropped. Since 1960, that median age has been steadily rising—up to twenty-eight years old in 2022.

One of the factors in the rise of midcentury marriages was political. The American tax code was changed in 1948 to favor married white couples, allowing them to file taxes jointly as one economic unit. However, this resulted in the lower earner now getting taxed at the higher-earning spouse's rate. Researchers say this was an attempt to get women out of the workforce, given that their wages were unlikely to outpace their husbands'. That's borne out by the historical record. Here's what good ol' Stanley Surrey, the author of the joint filing plan, wrote:

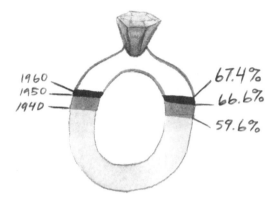

1960 67.4%
1950 66.6%
1940 59.6%

"Wives need not continue to master the details of the retail drug business, electrical equipment business, or construction business, but may return from their partnership 'duties' to the pursuit of homemaking."

What a guy!

It boggles the mind that we are still using this tax code to this day.

The 1950s was one of the rare times in American history when household breadwinners were predominantly male. Before this time, women often contributed to a family business and, before child labor laws, children contributed to the family income as well. In the 1950s Americans experienced an increase in wages for the first time in years. The increase of discretionary income raised the purchasing power of a household, leading to a flare-up in consumerism driven by new technology. It was easier than ever to be a homemaker thanks to new appliances like washing machines marketed entirely to women. (*See how fabulous this will make your life! You'll make your husband so happy with a clean home!*) But to puncture this fantasy bubble a little more, just because women could spend more time at home during this time doesn't mean they spent more time with their kids. Parents in 2012 spent more time with their kids than the parents of the mid-1960s, according to a study in *Journal of Marriage and Family*.

The 1950s ideal of marriage was born out of a perfect storm of factors according to Coontz. You have the end of World War II, which brought home many young men looking for stability, some tax code changes, more money in pockets—all these ingredients created just the right conditions for high rates of marriage. This midcentury marriage boom was not because people in the 1950s were better at loving or that "traditional marriage" was the pinnacle of romantic partnership. Traditional marriage never actually existed the way it's thought of today, and what did exist was, really, a blip in the history of marriage. Unfortunately, much of our American society is built around this historical speed bump. With a threadbare safety net, many parents today work multiple jobs in a punishing gig economy in hopes of chasing the single-earner "traditional" lifestyle that is increasingly harder to attain.

Coontz puts it best in her book: "It took more than 150 years to establish the love-based, male breadwinner marriage as the dominant model in North America and Western Europe. It took less than twenty-five years to dismantle it." This was thanks to, among other things, the women's liberation movement, more women in the workforce, accessible birth control, and general social progress.

Which brings us to today, when the number of people who never marry is on the rise. "Never marry," by the way, is a term used by the US Census. From 2006 to 2016, the number of never-married people between the ages of twenty-five and twenty-nine in America jumped from 45.6 percent to 59.7 percent. There's a similar jump for never marrieds in the next age group of thirty- to thirty-four-year-olds—from 26.2 percent in 2006 to 36.1 percent in 2016. Those are big jumps in just ten years. The gap between the number of never-married and married people is narrower than ever.

We also see many countries following a similar trend. As of 2017, the average age of a woman in Sweden at her first marriage was thirty-four years old, compared to twenty-eight years old in 1990. In Portugal, the average age in 2017 was roughly thirty years old, compared to twenty-four years old in 1991. There are countries where the average age of marriage remains quite low, but there does seem to be a larger global

MORE AMERICAN ADULTS ARE CHOOSING NOT TO MARRY

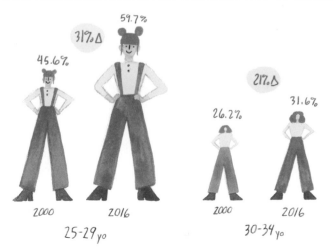

trend of women, in particular, waiting longer to get married. Globally, more women are also having children outside of the boundaries of marriage more often. In 2014, 65 percent of mothers in Mexico were not married at the time of their child's birth. The rate was 52 percent in Denmark, 35 percent in Germany, and 69 percent in Costa Rica in that same year.

There are many reasons why the number of never-married people is rising. Many of these people are in relationships and just, well, never married—perhaps because they can't afford to or because they just don't care to. These trends point to a new idea of "tradition," as far as I'm concerned, to be the "never marry" type who gets to live their life exactly as they see fit. It's time to let go of an ideal that never existed and see all the other valid ways to go through life.

Myth #5: Romantic love is the best kind of love.

There is entirely too much pressure put on romance. I don't even mean the pressure to woo someone with thoughtful romantic gestures. Anyone who's recently used a dating app can tell you the bar for *that* is in hell. I mean that society puts too much emphasis on romantic love as the bestest *best* kind of love out there—the kind of love that you should dedicate your life to finding and keeping or you'll end up sad and lonely.

I'm guessing if you're reading this book, you know that fairy tale is just that: fiction. And yet! Knowing all this unsavory history doesn't mean our ingrained notions of the supremacy of romantic love and marriage vanish. Nor does it keep a person craving connection from feeling disappointment and sadness when love doesn't happen exactly how they thought it would.

Although marriage rates do seem to be on the decline, many people still believe romantic love is the key to satisfaction in life. A 2019 Pew Research Center study reported that fewer than one in five Americans believe marriage is necessary for fulfillment, but one in four Americans believe being in a "committed romantic relationship" was essential to a fulfilling life. Twenty-six percent of respondents said that it was essential for men and 30 percent thought so for women. Essential! That's so demeaning to me. I know so many single people who are able to live rich lives with careers, friends, hobbies, and experiences. The lack of supposed essentialness of a partner doesn't seem to get in the way of having a fulfilling life.

We also expect a lot from modern marriage. Americans look to marriage to fulfill our personal growth and self-actualization needs, according to Eli Finkel at Northwestern University. When those needs are fulfilled, Finkel says that creates the conditions for the best marriages. But the problem is that more marriages don't clear that bar, which has increased rates of marital dissatisfaction. It's an all-or-nothing model of marriage, according to Finkel. That's a lot of pressure. How can any one person give you everything? It's an impossible standard to meet. Think about how different friends can provide different types of enjoyment in your life: Perhaps one friend is always up for a fun conversation about reality TV, another is always down to go deep emotionally, and another always has a great novel recommendation. It's natural for us to have different kinds of friends we can nerd out with about our specialized interests or with whom we have varying levels of intimacy. And yet, we still ask for all that and more from our partners.

There's even a term to describe our culture's obsession with romantic love: amatonormativity. It's a term coined by Elizabeth Brake, a professor of philosophy at Rice University. In her own words, amatonormativity means "the assumptions that a central, exclusive, amorous relationship is normal for humans, in that it is a universally shared goal." Brake notes that amatonormativity puts so much focus on monogamous romantic relationships that any other kind of relationship is seen as not as rewarding or worthy. This term is great to keep in your back pocket for the next time someone nags you about your love life. Look at them with pity and say, "That's really rather amatonormative of you."

But in all seriousness, amatonormativity is a helpful term. Language helps us give meaning to our experiences. Pinning that vague feeling that couples seem to rule the world to a specific word is almost a relief because it allows us to envision alternative realities that may be equally true. Amatonormativity captures the feeling that a wedding is a goal, that a husband or a wife is the aim, that we all should be striving for heterosexual, monogamous love, because it somehow makes us more moral. Living under amatonormativity means your worth and your goodness are dependent on your romantic relationship status.

This framework erases all the wonderful, varied kinds of connections that can and do exist. Amatonormativity relegates platonic friendships and the partnerships of folks who are queer, asexual, and/or polyamorous into "cultural invisibility." Any other relationship automatically takes a back seat: A group trip with friends is assumed to be flexible whereas the date of a wedding is ironclad; a single colleague may be expected to work late if a married colleague has an obligation with their spouse.

"Amatonormativity severely limits the concept of family."
— Elizabeth Brake

We also see this artificially inflated value of monogamous partnership in the expectations placed on single people with regards to how they spend their time and money. Single people are expected to attend as many weddings as they're invited to. It's an expensive obligation, to say nothing of the unpleasantness of being relegated to the singles table with the random solo cousins and coworkers. On group vacations, single people get stuck on the pull-out

couch or in a child's bed, often while being expected to pay the same share that the couples who get their own private rooms and bathrooms do. Single people are expected to prioritize the preferences of couples all the time. If we object to this unequal treatment, we are seen as difficult or selfish.

Brake also argues that amatonormativity severely limits the concept of family. That pesky nuclear unit keeps coming up, doesn't it? But it's everywhere. "One way of demarcating the privilege accorded by amatonormativity is that the privileged relationships are given family status," Brake writes. "Family tends to be understood, for legal and census purposes, either by marriage or a marriage-like relationship (such as monogamous cohabitation or 'common-law' marriage) or by the presence of children."

Families receive benefits that singles don't. Housing often discriminates against singles. You can often get more affordable health insurance if you're married. And amatonormativity is upheld in less formal ways, too. Think about how we talk about families socially; how people try to suss out your "family status" in social conversation. Brake gives this great example: When someone asks "Do you have a family?" at a dinner party, they don't mean "Do you have any siblings? Found family? A mother you care for?" No. They mean: "Do you have kids and are you married?" Sure, it's framed as polite conversation. But the assumption is telling about what our culture finds to be normal and acceptable.

To really shake us out of the romantic love spell, we might consider how evolutionary anthropologist Anna Machin defines love in her book *Why We Love*. According to Machin, love, in its crudest essence, is "biological bribery," where we are evolutionarily driven to mate for the perpetuation of the species, not to make us feel emotionally content and nourished. While it would have been lovely of evolution to drive us toward stable, mature partners who support us in pursuing our own interests and fulfillment, that's sadly not always the case.

Given all we know, there is more than a bit of absurdity in how we idealize romantic love. Perhaps it's time to think of love in a different way. Machin writes that after a decade of research, she is convinced that it is essential for humans to "re-engage with and celebrate the different types of love in our lives." Research shows that all strong relationships—not just romantic ones—benefit our health and well-being. "Any hierarchy of importance is a cultural construct," she writes. Our health and happiness are not dependent on partnership. We can gain the same benefits by maintaining good-quality relationships of all kinds. That means thinking of romantic love less as the highest peak and more as one of many on the fabulous, diverse spectrum of love.

On paper (perhaps this exact paper), all this seems lovely. Embracing more kinds of love sounds terrific! But I know it's easier said than done. There can still be a nagging sense of loneliness when you are single. Often, I would think to myself, *I know all the reasons why it's okay to be single, but I still feel sad I don't have a partner.* If this resonates with you, first remind yourself that humans are complicated; our emotions don't have to fit into a neat box. Multiple things about your life can be true at the same time and you can hold space for two seemingly opposing thoughts. You can love your freedom but also want companionship. There is room to want someone to share life with in a specific way and also room to know that a partnership is not the key to happiness. No one is grading you on perfect consistency.

But now that we know better, let's try to do better. Here are some activities, practices, and challenges to help these new, or reinforced, understandings about the limitations of love and marriage take root.

Art project: What does your own haze look like? Draw some of the different pressures you feel to be partnered. What kind of distracting, unhelpful phrases does the haze say to you?

PRACTICE

Think about all the different kinds of love in your life. Write down how these different relationships enrich your life.

Speak up for yourself! Not everyone is armed with what we now know about marriage. So when someone is being nosy about your personal life, feel free to respond with some of the following scripts:

So, are you dating anyone?

- "I don't feel like talking about it."
- "I'm not and am not looking right now."
- "No."

You're too picky!

- "Does that mean you weren't picky?"
- "I don't think I need to lower my standards just to be partnered."
- "I am picky. I deserve to be picky."

When are you getting married?

- "I don't know."
- "That's not a goal for me."
- "When are you getting married?"

- Or for the already married: "How is your marriage going?"
- Change the subject without blinking.

You know you'll find someone when you least expect it!

- "If that is true, how do I try to 'least expect it' now that I know this? Feels like a catch-22!"
- "I've got lots of other kinds of love in my life."
- "Okay! Good to know!"
- "I think it might just be luck and timing."
- "Why do I need to find someone?"
- "I don't feel like I need to wait for romantic love for my life to be fulfilling."

What happens if you use one of these prompts and you're still getting pushback? You have that one aunt who has a lot of advice about dating and a married friend who wants to set you up with their neighbor you have nothing in common with? Remember, these answers are all complete sentences and you don't owe anyone further explanations. Just because someone continues to pry doesn't mean you have to keep engaging on the subject. Be polite and direct and move on.

2

Shed the Stigma and Enjoy Yourself

IMAGINE YOU'RE ON A TREADMILL. YOU'RE jogging at a comfortable pace. You've got your water bottle, some tunes in your headphones. You're not technically going anywhere, sure, but you're moving. The first mile feels good and smooth, the second one, too. You're just about to wrap up after the three-mile mark when a message comes up on the monitor: "If you run three more miles, you'll get a prize!" Weird that this treadmill is giving out prizes, but who doesn't love a treat? You check your watch and shrug. You've got a little extra time today; why not?

So you keep running. You get that good feeling of pushing yourself in a workout but you're happy it's almost over. The six-mile mark flashes on the screen, but the treadmill doesn't slow down. "Update: The prize will be doubled if you run a little more!"

You're not sure what this prize is exactly but doubled is better, right? It'll all be worth it once you get that mystery double prize. But then the incline gets steeper and the tread-mill starts displaying messages like "You're still running? God, that's so sad. You must feel so lonely!"

The treadmill's messages come more rapidly:

"If you keep running alone, you're going to die alone."

"We just want you to stop running so you can finally be happy."

What the hell? you think. *I'm just trying to work out here! You told me to do this, you dumb treadmill!* A panic starts to rise in you. *I better get this prize—this seems serious.* You've lost count of the miles and you're out of breath. Enough. You straddle the treadmill to take a break. Your chest heaves. "Mission failed" scrolls across the treadmill's screen. "Here's what you would have won." An image of a diamond ring pops up. It kind of seems not your style, actually. Is it plastic? Wait a minute, you didn't even set out to win anything—but you ended up chasing something anyway.

Clearly this is my imaginary masochist's gym. Sure, it's a little dramatic, but this scenario replicates for me the feeling of being single in a culture that keeps throwing stigmas in your direction. You might be trying to just live your life, but these unwanted messages keep getting lobbed at you. For a long time, I was wrapped up in the many misconceptions about what it means to be single. Even though I considered myself a confident person, the sting of stigma was harder to overcome than I thought.

Our culture feeds us a toxic promise that we're always one promotion, purchase, or potion away from happiness. Once we get the object of our desire—a new apartment, a shiny award, a partner—we'll be satisfied. "But that's not how life works," says Jenny Taitz, clinical psychologist and author of *How to Be Single and Happy*.

Taitz calls this concept the "husband treadmill," a riff on the psychological effect called the hedonic treadmill or hedonic adaption. Typically, when we score that "prize," there's a momentary spike in

"The best way to change how you think is by changing how you live."

— Jenny Taitz

happiness, and then we more or less return to our happiness set point. That might seem a little depressing, says Taitz, but we can change where that baseline for happiness is set.

How? Essentially, you get off the treadmill. Stop the chase. For me, the longer I was on the hedonic treadmill, the more I engaged in corrosive behaviors like rumination and suppression.

Taitz says boosting our happiness set point is all about engaging in nourishing behaviors—things like mindfulness (more on that in chapter five) and pursuing positive activities that enrich our lives (a.k.a., enjoying the life you have now), all of which sounds much better than staying on a nightmare treadmill to nowhere.

In this chapter we will free ourselves from the stigma of singleness and meet ourselves. We will understand why the stigma singles carry is unjustified. We will explore practical ways to get comfortable with our own company. Being single doesn't mean being isolated, but it can mean longer stretches in your daily life of being on your own. If you're newly single or struggle with enjoying solitude, I'll offer some creative approaches to get you adjusted. It's time to learn to love the time you get to spend with you.

Singlism, the stigma of being single

Even if you can divest from the pressure to partner, it's hard to avoid internalizing the many harmful stories about singlehood. These negative perceptions are known as "singlism," a term coined by Bella DePaulo, a social scientist in the Department of Psychological and Brain Sciences at the University of California, Santa Barbara. Singlism, according to DePaulo, is "stereotyping, stigmatizing, marginalizing, and discrimination against people who are single." DePaulo has observed this phenomenon in her research—participants in one of her studies perceived singles as less well-adjusted and more selfish than their married peers. Ouch.

Singlism can be found everywhere, from dinner conversation with family to housing discrimination, from workplace dynamics to pop culture. Singlism renders the interests, dreams, and values of singles invisible, says DePaulo.

"Our interests don't matter if they don't involve trying to unsingle ourselves. Maybe we have passions that motivate us . . . or maybe we have careers we love, or maybe we contribute to our communities in meaningful ways," explains DePaulo.

"There is such a thing as loving single life and [it] is normal and natural and even commendable."

— Dr. Bella DePaulo

Society is deeply invested in having everyone coupled up. "In a way, the ideology makes an enticing promise—find The One, and all the pieces of your life will fall into place," says DePaulo. "Believing demeaning things about single people maintains the worldview that becoming married or coupled can transform your life for the better, turning sad singles into blissfully married people."

Singlism lurks in all the (frankly, tired) nasty sentiments thrown at single people.

DePaulo, through her research, has found that these negative perceptions are simply not true. Take the idea that single people are perpetually lonely. First, that assumption narrowly focuses on a single person's romantic relationship status. It discounts all other rich relationships in a person's life, like friends, relatives, colleagues, and mentors, says DePaulo.

And those non-romantic relationships do fill us up. Studies show that singles are more likely to have broader social groups—meaning they often have *more* friends and are more likely to contact and receive help from family than those who are married. Single people are active members of their communities and workplaces. Not having a romantic partner does not mean being cut off from all social connections.

DePaulo's work champions people our amatonormative society renders invisible: those she calls the single at heart. These are people who find that being single is "their most authentic, meaningful, fulfilling, and psychologically rich life." Being single at heart means not centering a romantic partner in your life and not wanting to, defying the stereotypes of singlism.

"One thing I have learned from studying people who are single at heart is that they are rarely lonely," says DePaulo. "That's because they savor solitude. Many single people who are not single at heart also experience loneliness no more often than anyone else."

Another common sentiment is that married people are always happier than singles. This idea is perplexing to me, given the many pop-culture depictions of marriage past the wedding as miserable. In countless movies, TV shows, and books both fiction and nonfiction, the hopeful excitement leading up to the wedding day—which comes with the pressure of it needing to be "the best day" of a person's life—is followed, apparently, by the drudgery. I'm thinking of all the sexist variations of "take my wife, please" and ball-and-chain jokes where a husband complains about his wife, and in return, the wife nags her useless husband. We get the contradictory messages that married people are happier even as our media portrays the long haul of marriage as a hard, inevitable struggle.

Of course, many happy marriages exist. But marriage is not a prerequisite for a joyful life. Studies show people who are in not-too-happy marriages have health equal to or worse

than those who are not married. DePaulo mentions that she's often heard that nothing is lonelier than being with someone who makes you feel alone. Not to mention that plenty of married people end up doing what so many others warn single people about: dying alone.

We know that being married doesn't necessarily make people happier. But marriage can feel like it has magical powers when you are yearning for something you don't have. That's what Elyakim Kislev, a faculty member at the Hebrew University and author of *Happy Singlehood*, found. His research showed that the more single people want a relationship, the less likely they are to be satisfied with their life.

If you're in that boat, hope is not lost. I know it isn't easy to just want something less. But instead of gritting your teeth and pretending you don't desire something, it's more helpful to turn your focus to what you like about your life right now and away from the future you can't control.

By giving singleness more of a chance, you might find that you enjoy it more than you anticipated. During the height of the pandemic, I became almost too good at enjoying my own company. I became pickier about how to spend my social energy and relished couch time with my dog over an overly full social calendar. I asked DePaulo if she thought it possible for a person to go from someone who longs intensely for a partner to becoming comfortably single at heart. She said that for some people, it can take time to become aware that being single is the best path for them because of the heavy emphasis on pairing up.

Many of these people try coupling up over and over again because they feel like it's what "normal" people do. "It comes as such a relief for them to learn that there is such a thing as loving single life and that it is normal and natural and even commendable," says DePaulo.

Building up gratitude

Liking your own company means focusing on what is good in your life right now. I've found that on the days I have low self-esteem, I can reroute my energy into noticing all the good experiences in my life. There are high points like going on a backpacking trip or seeing a Broadway show but there are also the everyday moments that make me feel grateful. Like the way the light filters through leaves and into my apartment in the morning or the joy of running into a friend on the street or the decadent taste of a fancy meal I made just for myself.

One powerful way to cultivate this sense of gratitude is to keep a journal for this purpose. Every day, simply write down five things you are grateful for—ice cream, a steady job, the way your pet makes adorable eye contact with you, your health, the fact that you woke up today. UC Davis gratitude researcher Robert Emmons found this kind of regular practice can lead to feeling more optimistic. Bonus: Emmons also found that the folks who kept a gratitude journal spent more time exercising and were even more likely to have a more optimistic view of their life.

You don't need to go into great detail about each thing you're grateful for, by the way. It's just as helpful to keep it short. I keep a running list on my phone. I get a warm burst of appreciation when I revisit it. Tiny moments of gratitude like this build upon themselves. I can't promise a gratitude practice will produce some quick, radical change in how you feel about your own company, but I can promise more moments of ease.

Depersonalize the angst

Okay, did you practice some gratitude, snap your fingers, and now you feel magnificent? I know, I know. This is all easier said than done, and I'm not telling you to not want what you want. I'm just proposing an alternative path where so much of your time and energy isn't devoted to this one pursuit.

But I understand how crappy it feels to want something and not have it. I would often find myself in this cycle: feel good about being single but think, why not date a little? So I would, and there would be the inevitable false starts, disappointments, and the not-quite-rights. I'd keep my head up, but after what felt like the millionth bland message from a dude on a dating app about how his weekend was—I'd crack.

What is wrong with me?

Before we go further, please know the answer is: *Nothing is wrong with you.* And know that that question did not even come from you. It was planted within you by a culture focused on a so-called ordered society of baby-making heterosexuals. That question feels so real, but it is an invasive message masquerading as self-reflection.

And yet, so many people find themselves asking it. After journalist Sara Eckel wrote *It's Not You: 27 (Wrong) Reasons You're Single*, she heard from people from all over the world who felt that sentiment deeply. Eckel's book tackles all the "societal muck" people throw at singles—fun, helpful sentiments like "You have too much baggage!" or "You're trying too hard!" It can be easy to rummage through these sentiments to pick out a specific diagnosis for yourself.

These messages all point to the idea that "if you're alone, there must be some reason. And that reason can't just be you haven't met the right person yet," Eckel explained to me. "It's gotta be you. It's gotta be something internal to you."

And if something is wrong with you, then, gosh darn it, you better fix it! It's all very much individualist thinking: Just pull yourself up by your single bootstraps. Eckel points out that this focus on "fixing" the single person gives a pass to all external and societal factors. Things like how different genders are socialized, the gamification of dating apps, and how the bar for a successful partnership is higher than ever, but the bar for basic kindness while dating is on the floor. For Eckel, it was helpful to focus less on what could be wrong with her and instead see the question itself as a reflection of these negative messages we've all been fed.

"If you feel lonely sometimes, that's okay."
— Sara Eckel

Here are some false reasons you may have received about why you're still single and how to reframe them:

"YOU'VE GOT ISSUES!"

Eckel remembers getting angry at a friend who said that unless she got "right with herself" she wouldn't find a partner. "And I got really mad at her and I was like, 'What do you think I've been doing this whole time?' And is every married person in the world this great bastion of mental health and esteem?"

There are no prerequisites for being in a relationship. Sure, there are healthy questions to ask before you couple up, but let's be honest, not everyone is doing that level of due diligence or working on their own personal growth. Great relationships aren't built between people who have handled their every personality flaw. They are made by finding someone who meshes well with you, says  Eckel. Release yourself from the notion that there is extra emotional work to be done before you become worthy of coupledom.

"YOU'RE TOO DESPERATE!"

Let's get straight to the point with this one: "A. No, you're not. And B. If you feel lonely sometimes, that's okay," says Eckel. We're social beings and didn't evolve to be alone, nor are we meant to be in isolated couples outside of a greater community. It's profoundly unfair that we are trained to want marriage and partnership, but if you admit that you might want that, something is wrong with you.

You're not desperate; you want connection. That is normal. (Are you noticing a theme?)

"YOU'RE TOO INTIMIDATING!"

Another classic. This statement is usually directed at high-achieving women who are successful in their careers or financial situations, to get them to downplay their accomplishments, to act demurer, in order to gain a partner. I fall into this allegedly "intimidating" category. After college, I started working at my dream company, NPR, producing podcasts like *TED Radio Hour* and *Invisibilia*, and eventually starting my own successful podcast, *Life Kit*.

I've unfortunately gone on too many dates with men who would assure me over drinks they had no problem with my success. They'd swirl an old-fashioned and offer up that they were the kind of guy who *loved* a strong, independent woman. The fact that they just volunteered this comment was always a bit of a red flag, and usually a sign that our time together was coming to an end. And, lo and behold, at the first suggestion of me picking up the check, they would disappear by the next day.

Eckel writes in her book that straight men are often given this convenient paradoxical standing. "They're presented as having all the power, at the same time we're told they're hothouse flowers, terrified of any woman who can fix a leaky faucet or unwind a credit-default swap."

For me, the easiest way to counter the idea that I'm too intimidating is to let those people be intimidated by me. It weeds out the people who can't hang. The right person will adore any accomplishments and status you've acquired.

My main takeaway from Eckel: What if instead of ruminating on all the negative reasons why you think you're single, you think of all the positive ones? Like you have a good intuition. Or you're independent, you like yourself, and you're not going to settle for a subpar relationship. We're all on our own paths, even if it gets hard to see them when there's so much in the way. But clearing the downed trees and overgrowth society puts in front of us can help us see where we're going more easily.

Perhaps consider that your singleness is a sign you're doing something right. There is nothing wrong with you. You can create peace for yourself.

Core beliefs

Even if you feel good and secure in your singleness, defending your position can be exhausting. Maybe you're happy going to a party solo, but one out of every ten times, you feel uncomfortable. The stigma around singleness can make the normal awkwardness of life jump to a darker place. An unpleasant moment can send you rocketing into "I'm unlovable" or "I'll never meet anyone" territory.

If that happens to you, slow down. Slow *way* down.

It might be helpful to unpack these core beliefs. In psychology, core beliefs are our personal assumptions of how we view ourselves, others, and the world around us. If you've got a core belief that humans are inherently good, then you're more likely to be patient with people. Conversely, negative core beliefs are going to give us a negative perspective.

What are the fundamental ways you view yourself? I have a feeling that there are plenty of positive core beliefs in there. But bad ones always seem to make the most noise. Notice when you fill in the blank of "I am _____" with something not so kind. Try in these moments to feed yourself an opposing thought. If "I'm unlovable" pops up, try responding with its opposite: "I'm lovable." Negative core beliefs limit your capacity to live with ease. How would your life look different if you didn't have that limiting belief about yourself?

"Changing your mind can only go so far," Taitz reminded me. "The best way to change how you think is by changing how you live."

The practice of flipping a negative core belief can help lead to positive change. One change I made was working to overcome my resistance to traveling without a partner. I thought I'd be too lonely drinking at bars alone or embarrassed trying to take selfies in front of tourist attractions. But I realized I don't have to travel completely solo. I planned a road trip through the Pacific Northwest, where my route took me to visit friends along the way. I organized a birthday trip to Portugal with my best friend, whose birthday is in the same month as mine (shout-out to Geminis—we are cooler than people realize). I signed up for a Costa Rican yoga retreat and made an effort to connect with other attendees. I made new friends by the end of the week. There wasn't anything lonely or sad about these travels—in fact, they created some of my favorite memories. I went from "I am self-conscious to travel because I'm single" to "I am amazing for traveling by myself."

Confronting your stigmatized thinking about singleness is helpful, but matching that with a behavior change is what really reshapes your internal narrative. "And not only does it change your narrative, even more importantly, it changes your life," Taitz says.

Combating singlism

We can all work on our singlism. In my experience, it takes self-awareness to first notice an assumption before you can behave differently. Pay attention to when you find yourself slipping into your own singlism—whether it's directed at you or another person—and try one of these suggestions from DePaulo:

- Ask single people what they love to do, what they enjoy most about their work, whether there's something they've done that makes them feel especially proud.
- Celebrate their accomplishments.
- Remember that a single person's life pursuits are just as important as those of coupled people.
- Show up for their birthdays and other important occasions.
- Ask your single friends and relatives about their friends, and their pets, if they have any.

- Recognize that plus-ones don't always have to be romantic partners.
- Understand that the deaths of close friends and relatives—and pets—can be devastating for anyone. If you are an employer, extend the same bereavement courtesies, considerations, benefits, and protections to your single employees as you do to your coupled employees.

Lonely vs. alone

So far we've gotten some insight into the way singlism shapes harmful narratives and how to unwind them. Now let's talk about embracing the joy of your own company. Because singles being perpetually lonely is a myth. This myth assumes that a person's single status precludes them from any love or connection—if they don't have a partner, they are basically in solitary confinement.

This myth also likes to conflate lonely and alone. It's important to dismantle this because mistaking one for the other can block you from enjoying time with someone pretty great: yourself.

To me, this stigma has a fundamental flaw. Because the most important relationship in anyone's life is the one they have with themselves. How we perceive, treat, and sit with ourselves determines how we show up for everyone else. Is spending time with ourselves that horrible? If we think being with ourselves is sad and lonely, what does that say about the kind of partner we would be? I want us to stop disrespecting the vital time everyone—single or partnered—needs in their own company.

I understand the pressure to avoid loneliness. First of all, it sucks to feel lonely! And there's evidence that not only is loneliness bad for you, it's also a killer. One study claims loneliness is as bad as smoking fifteen cigarettes a day. There's also evidence that social isolation is associated with higher risks of anxiety, depression, heart disease, and dementia. According to a 2023 US Surgeon General's advisory, even before the coronavirus pandemic, about half of US adults reported some measurable loneliness. But it's important to

note that feeling lonely sometimes is not the same thing as chronic loneliness. The advisory says that "chronic loneliness [even if someone is not isolated] and isolation [even if someone is not lonely] represent a significant health concern," but that "transient feelings of loneliness may be less problematic, or even adaptive." That's a helpful distinction. You can be a single person with a vibrant social life who experiences occasional bouts of situational loneliness. It doesn't mean you're automatically shaving years off your life.

Loneliness means being dissatisfied with being alone. It occurs when there is unhappiness about a lack of companionship or a perceived sense of social isolation. There are so many ways people can spend time alone without being lonely: reading a book, doing an art project, cooking a meal, or running errands. And there are plenty of ways people can be in relation with others and still feel lonely all the same, like when someone feels disrespected by their partner's behavior, when they feel like an outsider because of their identity or beliefs, or feeling misunderstood during a bad date that just isn't going anywhere.

This lonely/alone clarification helps destigmatize loneliness as a common human experience. According to the late professor and researcher John Cacioppo of the University of Chicago, loneliness is a biological signal akin to hunger or thirst. I find this conception of loneliness so helpful. When we are in a state of painful loneliness, it is our bodies giving us information to find social support or do reparative work on our self-love or social ties. You wouldn't be ashamed of needing water when thirsty, so why should you feel bad about feeling lonely?

In this framework, loneliness is a warning signal, but here is where it gets tricky. Oftentimes, people don't notice the buildup of the factors that make us feel lonely. According to Cacioppo, once those factors hit critical mass, your body starts to go into a self-preservation mode and creates what he calls "lonely social cognition." Loneliness causes us to be both more sensitive about our circumstances and less accurate in our thinking about them, causing us to look for (often false) evidence of threats. The more time spent in this hypervigilant state, Cacioppo says, the more likely you are to find yourself in the kind of spiral that degrades your health over time.

But there's no need to panic. Understanding the mechanics of loneliness already gets you halfway to dealing with it in a healthier way. Start to recognize when your brain is scanning for threats and heightening your emotional responses, like excessive anger about all those damn happy couples on the sidewalk or equating a date falling through to a massive flaw in your personality. Once you start to become more self-aware of those warning signals, you can respond by filling

your social and emotional cup. That doesn't mean you have to surround yourself with a big room of people. Connection thrives on quality over quantity—confiding in one thoughtful friend can help stop the loneliness spiral.

I won't downplay the serious ramifications of profound loneliness. And this is certainly not a call to just "get over" feeling lonely. If you haven't yet developed these coping tools, loneliness is not a switch that you can just flip off. But I do find there's relief in understanding that loneliness is a neutral signal—your well-meaning brain trying to protect you—and not some moral failing. My hope is this knowledge empowers everyone—single and partnered folks—to show up for themselves and others without judgment.

The joys of solitude

There are ways to transform the panic of loneliness into something more restorative. Just as being lonely isn't the same thing as being alone, solitude is its own flavor of alone time as well. Solitude is a neutral to positive state of being free of the demands of others. Solitude can be a beautiful respite. Sometimes you just want to eat cold pizza while catching up on *Shark Tank*—that's a beautiful thing!

While chronic loneliness is a threat to our health, solitude can be the opposite. You don't have to identify as an introvert to reap the benefits of solitude—it is for everyone. Even just fifteen minutes of solitude can help you regulate your emotions. Solitude also provides the space for creative thinking to happen. And perhaps most importantly, finding time for solitude can help you gain deeper self-knowledge. For me, moments of self-insight often arrive when I'm taking a solo walk. I experience these insights like a butterfly landing gracefully on a flower—so beautiful and almost impossible to notice until I slow down enough to see it in the first place.

Liking your own company

If you have picked up a book about single life, it's very possible you're already a pro at alone time. Congrats! I'm proud of you. Bella DePaulo describes being able to savor, even crave, solitude as a superpower. If you're already experienced at recharging in solitude, the following suggestions are offerings to help deepen your solitude practice.

If you're nervous about the idea of even spending a moment alone with your thoughts, not to worry. You're already doing step 1, which is learning about the benefits of solitude. One study found even doing just that can help shift negative beliefs about alone time. Next, think of all the things you already do on your own. Do you worry that someone will judge you for going solo to pick up a prescription at the pharmacy? No! You're just a person getting shit done.

Single stigma doesn't come up in this example partly because there's no social expectation that you need to do errands with someone. According to research by Rebecca

Ratner, a marketing professor at the University of Maryland's Robert H. Smith School of Business, the public nature of an activity shapes how someone makes the decision to do that activity. Ratner found people are more likely to prefer to go to a movie with a friend on a Saturday night, a time often sanctioned for socializing, but are more open to going to a movie alone on a sleepy Sunday. Personally, I love going to a movie by myself and have never felt weird about it. You're in a dark room facing a screen, not talking with people. In my opinion, it is the perfect solo activity for any time.

That's why it bums me out that Ratner also found that people often avoid activities they enjoy if they have to do them alone, especially if they would be observed doing them in public. Look, life is short. Why deny yourself the distinct pleasure of seeing a film on discount night followed by a delightful solo walk home just because someone might think you're single? (Just me?)

Ratner also found that people tend to *underestimate* how much they will enjoy a solo activity. Sometimes hanging with people is a drag! You have to make compromises about how much money to spend or what kind of food to eat or how long you're going to be out. But when you carve out delicious moments for just you—taking yourself shopping, hiking, roller-skating, whatever it is—you get to be the sole architect of your experience. There can be a certain air of romance to the time you give yourself.

Here are some ideas for tailoring solitude, depending on your personality.

IF YOU'RE NERVOUS ABOUT SPENDING TIME ALONE:

 Not everyone loves a discount Tuesday night movie the way I do. Spending time alone, for some, is boring. The reason boredom can make us feel antsy, according to one theory, is because we are looking to engage in an activity without knowing what to latch on to.

Reduce the pressure of needing to fill your alone time with something exceptionally stimulating or thrilling, and start by getting used to smaller bouts of solitude. You don't need to block off a whole weekend in a cabin in the woods or jump straight to a solo dinner at a busy restaurant. Start practicing in the comforts of your own home.

Try putting your phone on airplane mode and set a timer for twenty-five minutes to do something absorbing. I suggest doing something with your hands like an art project, cooking, or gardening. That way, you'll be lost in the flow of the activity and not obsessing over whether you're doing solitude right. When your timer goes off, take a five-minute break. Feel free to check your texts or scroll social media for a moment. Then, try another twenty-five-minute burst of solitude. This approach is known as the Pomodoro Technique, a great method for studying or focused work. I also like to use this method for any task that I'm dreading because once I'm lost in the task, I often want to keep my momentum, and may even skip the break altogether. Don't feel bad if that flow doesn't happen right away. Right now you're just working to increase your tolerance for solitude. The hardest part is showing up.

IF YOU'RE LOOKING TO CHANNEL YOUR CREATIVITY:
Solitude doesn't have to be something to do just because it's good for you. You can give it a more concrete purpose. One potential goal: increasing creativity. There's plenty of research to suggest that solitude can help fuel creative thinking.

I have to admit something. While I identify as a creative person, I'm quite type A. I like structured boxes of time in which to write or do crafts, and I dislike straying too far from a neat plan, which is not a very bohemian-artist-living-in-a-loft sort of vibe. But I've realized that if I set aside my self-consciousness about being an uptight creative person, I can find beauty in the structure I crave. Creating expected times for creativity gives me 1) restorative solitude, 2) regular opportunities to do creative projects, and 3) momentum to continue seeking creativity. If you're longing to stretch your creative muscles and nervous about spending too much time alone, bundling your creative time with solitude could be the trick.

One popular technique comes from Julia Cameron's classic book *The Artist's Way*. It's a simple practice aimed at sparking your creativity but it also helps generate meaningful solitude. At the heart of *The Artist's Way* is the practice of morning pages. The concept is straightforward: Every day when you wake up, you write three pages in longhand. It doesn't have to be perfect prose. In fact, it likely won't be. You could write about what you're going to do that day, what you did yesterday, a recipe you're looking forward to making, or your feelings about a television show. I sometimes get meta with it and write, "I feel like I have nothing to say but I am moving my hand across the page." It doesn't matter what you write. You're just getting in the habit of putting pen to paper and creating imperfect output. For me, showing up for this kind of practice helps unlock little insights I didn't know were in me. Even if you're not trying to write a novel, morning pages can be a fantastic way to spend thirty minutes with yourself.

Cameron's other signature suggestion, an artist date, is another great way to try creative solitude. The artist date is a solo activity of what she calls "assigned play." It's a way to explore something that interests you to gather creative inspiration. This could be wandering through an art supply store to look at materials or hitting up a museum exhibit. (Fun fact: One study from Rebecca Ratner suggests people tend to enjoy a solo visit to an art gallery as much as if they went with a friend. Maybe being with others means folks are often too caught up making sure they are having a fun time to absorb the art itself?)

Your artist date doesn't have to be in a place dedicated to capital-A Art. It could be sifting through postcards at a vintage shop or going to a park on the other side of town just to look at some different flowers. Artist dates are meant to provide new input for your creativity. Something I love about this kind of solitude is that it pushes me to sprinkle a little bit of novelty into my life. It can be so easy to fall into a pattern (for me, at the moment, it's *Real Housewives of Potomac* while scrolling TikTok on commercial breaks after a long workday).

But using my alone time for an artist date breaks me out of the cycle and often ends up energizing me.

IF YOU LIKE DOING A PROJECT:

During the pandemic, I missed going to the movies. For me, nothing beats settling down in a dark theater with a box of Junior Mints straight from the fridge. Unable to go to my favorite local theater, I couldn't recreate that exact experience, so I made up a little challenge for myself to watch as many movie trilogies as possible. I dove into the Richard Linklater *Before* films, the *Back to the Future* trilogy (weirdly, I had never seen these growing up), the *Matrix* movies, and more. Sure, this self-assigned project got me caught up on movies that had been on my to-watch list, but it also helped solve the question of "what the hell am I going to do with all this alone time?"

Work your way through a cookbook à la *Julie & Julia*. Commit to trying out a new biking path once a month. Train for a 5K. Try out a new coffee shop every weekend. Spend time reading all the books of your favorite author. Write a short story a day for a month. Design a project around something you enjoy and then block time for it in your schedule. Folding activities into a routine increases our chances of actually doing them. If I know that once a week on Sunday afternoons I want two hours of writing time for this book—it's going on the calendar. I've already made the decision that it's happening. Will there be Sundays when I won't honor this commitment? Sure will. But that creative solitude happens more often because I explicitly add time for it in my routine.

IF YOU THRIVE WITH OTHERS:

Even a "people person" needs solitude. And you can use that propensity for socialization and community to your advantage. You can reimagine your solitude time as a sort of prep session for cultivating your connections. Yale psychologist and research scientist Emma Seppälä's work on compassion and social connection found that the benefits of social connection—higher self-esteem, better emotional well-being, increased chance of longevity—come from a person's "internal and subjective sense of connection."

To me, that relieves some of the pressure to be social every day. Instead, you can use your alone time to do things that boost your sense of *internal* connection. There's research that suggests doing good deeds for others is more effective at raising our happiness levels than doing something for ourselves. You might drop off a meal for a friend going through a tough time. Make homemade birthday cards. Plan out an itinerary for an upcoming friend excursion.

You can also strengthen a sense of connection in your solitude through loving-kindness meditation. This is a type

 of meditation (supported by research and a long Buddhist tradition) aimed at cultivating a sense of compassion not only toward yourself, but also toward those around you. It's also a

great habit for combating hope-
lessness and self-criticism.

There are many different
styles of loving-kindness meditation but here's one to get you
started, adapted from mindfulness expert Sharon Salzberg:

1. Set yourself up in a seated position, eyes closed if you
   wish.

2. Bring yourself to mind. Repeat these phrases to yourself:

   May I be happy.
   May I be healthy.
   May I be safe.
   May I live with ease.

3. Feel free to change these phrases if they feel awkward
   at first. Tailor them so they best evoke a sense of compassion and gratitude within you.

4. Next, bring to mind someone you love who's shown
   you care. Repeat the same phrases directed toward
   them.

5. Bring to mind someone who's an acquaintance. Repeat
   the phrases.

6. Think of someone you have difficulty with or who
   you find frustrating. Send them loving-kindness with
   the phrases.

7. Go further and extend beyond your community. Bring to mind all living beings. Send all in the universe loving-kindness with the phrases.

For me, loving-kindness meditation creates invisible strings of connection to those in my life. I often finish a session feeling not only calmer, but less lonely. I feel like my soul is sending out little paper planes of love to people. It's not just some spiritual alchemy happening here—loving-kindness meditation has been found to increase positive emotions like joy, awe, and hope. That snowballs into other positives like a greater sense of purpose and social connection.

A note on all this solitude

I'm a cheerleader for solitude, but I acknowledge it is not always wonderful. In upcoming chapters we'll explore managing big emotions and runaway thoughts that can come up when we're alone, but for now it's important to say: You do not always have to enjoy your alone time. Think of it like any other social interaction. Sometimes brunch out with friends is all laughs and the energy is just right. But other times someone complains a little too much about their job or their ex and the vibe is off. Some days, solitude will not feel joyous. There will be times you feel antsy, bored, or just plain lonely. Sit with those feelings of discomfort when they come. Ask yourself what need this discomfort is pointing to and what you could change to meet it. If you know some of your loneliness triggers, plan ahead. Make proactive plans for the long holiday weekend when everyone you know always seems to take couples trips. Lock in your winter travel plans early. There is always flexibility in how you navigate your experiences. But with regular practice and an open mind, you will hopefully find yourself looking forward to your alone time more and more.

ACTIVITY

Pick your style of solitude.

- Are you looking to increase your creativity? Cultivate a better connection with your loved ones? Tackle a project or just acclimate to the tiniest stretch of alone time? Select your solitude style and schedule dedicated time for it.

Keep a gratitude list.

- You can keep it short and sweet. Take one minute to list out five things you're grateful for every day. Try to think of new ones each day. Challenge yourself to go beyond some of the basics (a home, a job, your health) if you feel like you're repeating yourself. Sometimes noticing the small delights of life (the way two dogs run up to each other on the sidewalk and then pause when they get nose-to-nose—one of my recent examples) helps to inspire more opportunities for gratitude.

Take proactive measures to squash negative associations you have with singleness.

- If seeing an ex-partner on social media makes you spiral, block them. In fact, block their current partner, if they have one, while you're at it.

- If you have a loved one who gives you terrible dating advice if you even so much as mention your singleness, don't bring up dating or romance. Don't give them the opportunity to play old tapes about why you should be doing one thing or another to land a partner.

Combat singlism wherever you go.

- Remember that singles are whole human beings. Engage both yourself and other singles in discussions about their interests, goals, and hobbies. Acknowledge that singles can have fulfilling relationships outside of romantic ones. Don't assume that singleness is a waiting room.

Stop comparing yourself. For real.

- When you feel the urge to compare—whether it's with a friend who's always meeting new people at bars or your sister who's got a supportive husband and a baby on the way—take some inventory. Was there a clear prompting event that made you want to compare yourself to someone else? Was it something you saw on social media? Was it a particular phrase? Dissect the chain of events that led you to this negative association. Then ask, "Is this thought helping me?"

3

Living Inside Your Own Head

STORIES ARE IMPORTANT TO ME AS A WRITER, journalist, and arts lover. Love me some beginning, middle, and end. Stories are not only entertaining; they also help us make sense of the world. But I've found that when it comes to my personal life, I can get a little too attached to a story and it can get me into trouble.

For a long time, I told myself the story that I was the "rebound girl." That people only dated me when they needed to get over a seemingly bigger and more important relationship that had ended right before we met. I was there with the dustpan ready to sweep up all the pieces and put them together again, only to find *myself* broken into tiny bits shortly thereafter when our sudden breakup inevitably followed.

Why do I keep ending up in these situations? Why am I attracted to these kinds of men? Why do people only want to date the early-in-the-relationship me? Why do I keep getting rejected? Why doesn't someone want to be with me?

I started to reach for the "rebound girl" story more frequently. After receiving another dreaded "I've had a really fun time hanging out with you but . . ." text from a four-date wonder, I'd turn to the story. The theme of "rebound girl" was rejection, so it seemed to fit any number of disappointments.

I'd crack open that damn story for anything. A boring date with someone I felt zero chemistry with? Another chapter in the *Tales of the Rebound Girl*. Invited to yet another wedding with no plus-one? Let's see where we left off in our story. A flash of a memory of a past relationship? Fire up the never-ending story I hate. But I revisited it constantly, thinking there was a key in there somewhere to what I was missing.

I must be broken, cursed, unlovable. People just leave me, that's what it is; I'm a leaveable person.

All these negative thoughts made me miserable. But since I spent all this time thinking about and analyzing my story, I thought it must be the truth, that these thoughts were the only conclusions to draw. It took time to realize that I wasn't feeling horrible because this story was true—but

because I was thinking about it constantly. I had made a little reading nook in my brain where I only read that specific story to myself. I didn't know how to live in my own head without ruminating on this narrative.

Thankfully, it's possible to choose different stories. In this chapter, we delve into our thoughts. We'll discuss how rumination works and strategies for combating overthinking. Because getting lost in a negative thought loop doesn't have to be inevitable.

The backstory on thoughts

When we experience something uncomfortable, our natural instinct is to bat it away. To only seek out comfort. Sometimes I overthink how much easier my life would be if I didn't overthink so often—helpful!—or maybe if I didn't think much at all. But thinking—deeply thinking—is necessary and wonderful in so many ways.

Thinking is a crucial adaptive tool for humans. It allows us to reflect on our past, learn from mistakes, and savor experiences. We use thinking to plan for the future, protect ourselves, and provide for ourselves and loved ones.

But like with any tool, it requires skill to use it to its fullest potential. How we pay attention to our thoughts and how we interact with them has a big impact on our moods and self-view. Repetitive negative thinking can be a common symptom of anxiety and depression. A 2013 study from psychology and neuroscience researchers Florence J.M. Ruby and Jonathan Smallwood found that thinking about the past can lead to negative moods—even if the content of the thoughts was positive. In contrast, they found future-oriented thoughts could lead to a more positive mood, even if the thoughts were negative. We'll get more into managing emotions in the next chapter, but for now let's pop open the hood of the brain for a moment so we can understand the biological mechanics of what we call thinking.

Enter: the prefrontal cortex. It's the brain's executive function center. It regulates thoughts, emotions, and action by connecting to other parts of your brain. If you've ever made too many mental to-do lists in your head while also trying to text your friend and finish up a work email, you know that it's easy for your prefrontal cortex to get fatigued. Adding another task to your overworked prefrontal cortex's plate, like, say, repetitive thinking about why someone you liked rejected you? You're going to be pretty mentally fried.

"What some people often don't realize is that the process of overthinking things actually consumes your executive functions," explains Ethan Kross, professor of psychology and management at the University of Michigan and author of *Chatter: The Voice in Our Head, Why It Matters, and How to Harness It*.

"At a certain point in the conversation . . . broaden your perspective."

— Ethan Kross

Overthinking takes up the same mental resources we need to get us out of the rumination loop. A horrible cognitive catch-22. Who approved this design?

Sometimes we are lucky and we can untangle the negative thoughts quickly and move on. But sometimes overthinking leads to more anxious, catastrophic thinking. Here's how Dr. Judson Brewer, psychiatrist and director of research and innovation at Brown University's Mindfulness Center, puts it: fear + uncertainty = anxiety.

Uncertainty adds fuel to the fire. The complete uncertainty of not knowing when or if the right partner might come into your life can feel distressful. Add in past negative experiences, triggers (say engagement photos on Instagram or a failed flirting attempt), an attachment to a negative belief (*being single sucks*), and well-worn habits of overthinking and overanalyzing and, well, "that's like a very dry forest ready to blaze," says Brewer.

"We can't change something that happened in the past, but we can change the future by how we behave . . . and how we think."

— Dr. Judson Brewer

This is because human brains thrive on knowing information. When you're faced with a problem—let's say you're worried about striking a balance between time for dating and time for hobbies—the prefrontal cortex looks up your past experiences for a solution. It might think, "Got it! I know the last time I was worried about spending too much energy on dates, I scheduled more time to rock climb. I can relax! I know how this is going to go." But when your prefrontal cortex doesn't have enough good information—like if you're worried about when a potential life partner might show up—it will still

The Habit Loop

look for that information even if it doesn't exist. In the quest to satisfy that craving for certainty, the brain starts spinning potential scenarios in preparation. But constant mental rehearsals don't make us feel better. In fact, they backfire.

A state of panic is a state of unthinking.

This mental habit is no fun, but we can get stuck there. Brewer calls these habit loops. They break down to:

1. Trigger
2. Behavior
3. Result

These habit loops work perfectly with our brain's reward-based learning system. When you're hungry (trigger), you seek out food (behavior), and then you're satisfied (result). Problems arise when the result is something not so rewarding. Swiping all night on a dating app might feel like you taking charge of your dating life, but likely it just makes you feel bad. Plus, excessive rumination can keep our bodies in a chronic state of activated stress. During an overthinking session, I become hypervigilant (*I think this person is going to stop texting me*, I told myself with no real evidence that this would be the case). And while stress isn't inherently bad (it can help us identify and avoid dangerous situations), it also steals resources from other important processes that should be taking place in the body in order to keep us healthy.

So why do we engage in these ultimately unrewarding activities?

For one, it gives people a sense of control, Brewer told me. But this so-called sense of control acts like empty calories. It's feeling like you're doing something (which feels better than doing nothing), but it's also not a truly helpful activity. These habit loops can also be a result of trying to protect your sense of identity. A 2016 study by psychologist Jonas Kaplan at the University of Southern California found that when people were confronted with contrary evidence about their political beliefs, participants who were most resistant showed greater activity in a part of the amygdala (associated with processing threats, fear, and anxiety), a part of the insular cortex (which processes data in decision-making), and the default mode network (which activates when we ruminate and is connected to our sense of self). Essentially, our brains are reluctant about changing our beliefs about our sense of

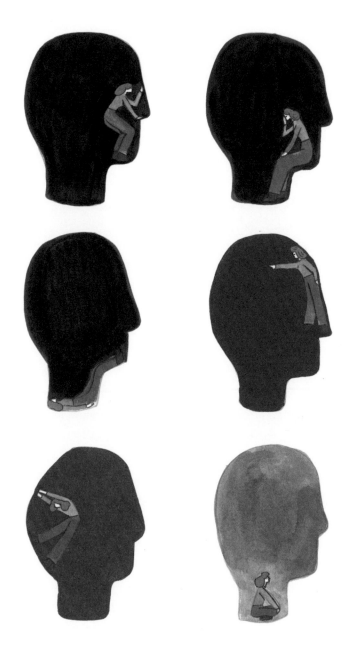

self, which can lead to overthinking and emotion. "We don't think our findings are particular to political beliefs, but any belief that is identity related," Kaplan told me. That means if you think that you shouldn't be single, but you keep going on boring dates and it feels like a conspiracy against you, that's your brain working to protect your beliefs about yourself.

Understanding rumination

There's an important difference between repetitive thought patterns and rumination—the former isn't inherently bad. My wandering brain loves to return to the same low-stakes subjects again and again: my ever-evolving skincare routine, the leftovers in my fridge and how I can transform them for dinner, what could be happening in a parallel universe at this very instant. Even if I don't know the answer to these questions right away, I can typically come to a stopping point and move on with my day. Rumination starts when our brains can't move on, according to Edward Watkins, a professor of experimental and applied clinical psychology at the University of Exeter and author of *Rumination-Focused Cognitive-Behavioral Therapy for Depression*, a training manual for therapists.

It's natural to want to think through a problem. The trouble starts, Watkins says, when we need to understand every possible detail of a question before we can take an action. A question like, oh, I don't know, why you might still be single?

Rumination is a particular flavor of repetitive thinking. It involves dwelling on something repeatedly, while often blaming ourselves in the process, all of which leads to negative emotional consequences. Instead of being a productive, self-reflective space where your thinking can lead to break-throughs, rumination not only encourages you to keep mulling over a topic, but it takes (get this) you further away from any kind of solution. Watkins illustrates the difference with this example in his book: You're having car trouble. You might think, *The battery must be dead—this is so frustrating!* or you could think, *Why is this happening to me?*

There are a few differences between these thoughts. The first one is nonpersonal. It's rooted in reality and prompts you to think about next steps to fix the situation. The second thought doesn't have anything to do with the fact that your car likely needs a jump.

"The trouble starts when we need to understand every possible detail of a question before we can take an action."

— Edward Watkins

Instead, it primes you to get lost in larger existential and negative questions that are not going to get your car moving. This both slows down your day and affects how you feel about yourself. Watkins says "why" questions are a hallmark of rumination, according to his research.

You know the kind—*why me?* These questions feel valid and worthy of trying to answer. But many times, instead of

unearthing a revelation, a "why" question just keeps us asking more questions. There are endless ways to fill in the blanks. Trying to answer those questions causes the problem in front of us to morph into something more abstract as a result, says Watkins.

Abstract problems are famously hard to solve and can leave us in that not-so-fun place of fear and uncertainty. Cue the sadness, anxiety, and frustration. Then come more catastrophic thoughts like *Something about me is wrong.* Catastrophic thinking is often untrue and, what's more, it prevents the conditions needed for more nurturing, helpful thoughts.

The sneaky part about rumination is how it *feels* like it's problem-solving. A study by psychologists Sonja Lyubomirsky and Susan Nolen-Hoeksema found that when a group of depressed people spent eight minutes overthinking, they felt like they'd gained insight about their lives, but they hadn't actually made progress. I can't tell you how many times I've ruminated about a past hurt and thought something like, "I'm *this* close to figuring out why this person dumped me out of the blue! Then I can finally stop thinking about it!" But ruminating isn't asking reality-based questions with factual answers—it's just easier to spin my wheels instead of dealing with the pain.

When you want to ask a "why" question, try flipping it into a "what" instead. Try "what can I do differently?" instead of "why am I so unhappy?" Think "what might make me feel better right now?" instead of "why am I feeling so alone?" That small shift can help negative thoughts feel more manageable.

The tricky thing about venting

When negative thoughts are bouncing off the walls of my mind, it makes sense to let them out. Aren't friends and loved ones supposed to lend a supportive ear when we're frustrated about something in our lives? Venting feels like a good option, right?

Sadly, not quite. Venting is also known as co-rumination. It can feel good at first since you might get some validation—it *is* annoying to reschedule that first date for the third time!—but there is lots of evidence to show that venting doesn't have the positive effect it seems like it should. Let's be honest, when's the last time you vented for a long time and truly felt relieved after? Did you fully expel that demon thought from your brain and never return to it? Unlikely.

A study by Kross and his colleagues found that participants venting frustrations via online communication were more likely to have their negative feelings linger. One theory suggests that venting our anger can prime us to respond with aggressive thoughts, feelings, and behaviors in the future. In my experience, seeking out people to vent to about the same issue tends to cement an exaggerated version of the story. Not to mention, you risk burning out your friends and family if you keep rehashing the same topics.

Look, venting is a very natural instinct. When we're having big feelings and thoughts, we want to connect with others who can validate our feelings. There's a reason many rants start with "Can I get a gut check on this?" I'm not saying that you should never vent to a loved one about something that's bothering you, but try to think of it only as a first step. Kross says after venting, two critical stages need to follow: support and perspective shifting.

For support to be helpful, it has to be constructive. There are two main traps your co-ruminating crew can fall into: 1) Those who, while meaning well, rev you up to vent even more, but do nothing to help you see your situation rationally, and 2) those who get too clinical with their problem-solving efforts (*"You're frustrated about being*

single? Why don't you just join a dating app? I did that and that's how I met my partner! Just do that and I'm sure it'll be fine." Extra negative points for oversimplification and patronizing demeanor.). Both of these types of support are likely to leave you feeling worse than when you began.

Before you vent to someone, you first want to think about whether this person is a good "chatter advisor," as Kross puts it. "You want people who do take the time to hear you out, to empathize, validate your experience, and so forth. But at a certain point in the conversation, they start working with you to help broaden your perspective." There's a bit of an art to that.

HERE'S WHAT THAT CAN LOOK LIKE:

- "I know this is difficult for you now. But I believe in your ability to find the right path."
- "You're right. That is hard. But I also want you to remember what is good in your life."
- "I hear you. I'm sorry you're going through that. I know in a few months this will be a distant memory but I'm here for you now."
- "Do you need validation right now—because you're right that this is hard—or do you want some advice?"
- "I know you feel like this always happens, but I remember a few weeks ago when you went through something similar. You got through it then; I know you can get through it now."

Think about who's naturally good at this in your life. Really think critically about who's good at comforting and validating, but also good at giving you that gentle bit of reality. Seek them out when you want to get something off your chest. Maybe that means it's time to stop leaning on that one friend who tells you it's all crap and there are no good people out there these days. Or maybe stop venting to your married-with-three-kids brother who jumps into savior mode and has no experience with the shitty realities of modern dating. You deserve to be picky about who your venting partners are.

Breaking the cycle

Addressing rumination is a worthy effort.

Different approaches work for different people. Mix and match these tools to create your own kind of cerebral cocktail, one that will clear your cognitive state instead of blur it. Also, I want to note that these are not meant to be (and could not be!) the only solutions for overthinking, nor will these treat clinical mental health issues. If you're dealing with a mental health diagnosis, please see a mental health professional for medical advice.

Our goal here is not to get rid of any negative thoughts at all. It's to work with your thoughts and not get swept away by them. In a way, you've already started this process if you're aware of your rumination. "The first thing is you need to spot the cues to the habit, what's setting it off," says Watkins. "Because otherwise it's just going to keep happening without you being aware of it."

1. TRACK THE OVERTHINKING.

Let's start with some cognitive behavioral therapy (CBT) techniques. Start keeping a rumination journal. This can be a note in your phone or a physical notebook or diary. When you notice you're slipping into a runaway thought or some of those pesky "why" questions begin swirling, stop and make note of it. I like to write down the date, the time, the nature of the thought, and what I was doing when the thought arose. You can also note roughly how long you ruminated for or what kind of emotions come up. Watkins told me that if you're spending about thirty minutes or more ruminating about a topic, it's typically a sign you dwell too long.

After about a week of logging, see if any patterns emerge. For example, I found that my daily commute to work was high tide for rumination. I took the same route each day, meaning I was mostly on autopilot, and since I didn't have to spend mental energy figuring out my next turn, my mind instead turned to ruminating (the world's worst podcast). The tracking taught me to be aware that commuting was a minefield for me, so I came up with a menu of options to divert my thinking: taking a different path, calling my mom, noticing all the lovely DC row houses, or even just making a point to be aware of each step I was taking. Of course, I would sometimes slip up and slide back into ruminating over old fights with ex-boyfriends—complete with imagined full takedown monologues fit for a prestige drama—but even when I fell off the wagon, the journal helped ground me in reality: *Look at all the time I've spent thinking about this. Is this really how I want to spend my time? Is this making me feel better at all?*

Tracking is a good place to start, but perhaps you're an expert level ruminator like myself. In that case, you likely need some other options.

2. DISRUPT YOUR ENVIRONMENT.

Perhaps bedtime is overthinking time for you. You may lie in bed and, instead of resting, your mind is making a mental list of every person who's ever wronged you, what you might be missing out on when your friends go on double dates, how you're ever supposed to buy a house with just one salary in this economy, and, oh my god, what are you even doing with your life?

Not exactly conducive to a good night's sleep!

"There you really want to break that link between being in bed and thinking by doing something else," says Watkins. When the rumination starts and you're tossing and turning, the key is "getting up and not lying there, breaking that association." This is a similar technique used to treat people with insomnia—you get out of bed if you can't fall asleep and only return when you're tired enough to do so. Changing up your environment when encountering a trigger can be helpful.

You can also try immersing yourself in nature. While not everyone can escape to a national park every time a rumination loop hits, the good news is research shows even small doses of nature like a walk down a tree-lined street can help us relax. Experiencing awe gives us a sense of "perceived vastness," according to Dacher Keltner, a psychologist at the University of California, Berkeley. That sense of being in the presence of something larger than ourselves helps quiet our

nervous system and inner critic. You can also access awe by witnessing the good in others. Keltner finds that keeping your eyes peeled for the moments of "moral beauty" can lead to awe, like an act of kindness between strangers. Even seeking out inspiring speeches or writing can have the same beneficial impact.

3. RESPOND DIFFERENTLY TO THE TRIGGER.

Sometimes changing up your environment isn't an option. Another CBT tool is to learn to respond a different way when you're presented with a rumination trigger. Low mood commonly sets off worry. If your habit is to ruminate when you're feeling sad, then you're likely to stay in that cycle. An alternative response to a trigger helps break that link.

That alternative response to low mood could be practicing self-compassion or engaging in an absorbing activity. (Remember how that was a great option for tapping into the benefits of solitude? It's a mental health BOGO deal.) Sewing, reading, dancing, baking—whatever keeps you in the moment and feeling good. These kinds of activities keep you grounded instead of whisked away on a train of thought. One study found that giving people with depression a distraction for as little as eight minutes lifted their mood. Think about that— you could be less than ten minutes away from feeling better.

Try the same approach with venting. Maybe you vent for a bit, but when you start to actively scroll through your contact list to see who else you can vent to (example not based on personal experience . . .), catch yourself and do something different.

In those moments, ask yourself, "What is it that you want in an interaction? What is it that you need in an interaction?" says clinical psychologist Jenny Taitz. You don't need to go full-on positivity or ignore the reality of your situation. But if you're caught in a worry spiral, Taitz says that points to you needing a break. Instead of a venting session, ask your friend to go to karaoke or pick up some novels at your favorite bookstore. Actively decide to do something different than spending time psychoanalyzing a text from a date. Instead of putting a Band-Aid on your negative thoughts by co-ruminating, nourish yourself with a positive social experience.

4. PROBLEM-SOLVE.

I know I just talked about how rumination isn't actually problem-solving. And it still isn't! But there is a trick to thinking through problems without getting totally lost in the fog.

First, let's do some reverse engineering. Unresolved goals often stoke the flames of rumination, says Watkins. If your goal is to have a partner and you don't have one, you're going to feel restless about that unresolved goal. A romantic relationship hinges on timing and

luck and, most crucially, another person. And if you've ever done a group project, you know other people aren't always dependable.

Instead of thinking of partnership as the end goal, get under the surface of that desire. Do you crave connection and community? Maybe you can sign up for a class you'd enjoy or volunteer for a cause you believe in. Looking for peace? Maybe you can spend more time in nature or take up a meditation practice. Try to think of ways you can make the underlying goal something *you* can give yourself. Turning your unresolved goal into a realistic one can focus that over-thinking energy.

Ask yourself: What's the thing I can do today to take me to the next step? "The more you're taking concrete steps, the more likely it is that things are going to go in the right direction," says Watkins. Perhaps you've been waiting to do more traveling until you have a romantic partner to go with. Instead, take the first step now toward planning that weekend camping trip with friends or that road trip across the country. Otherwise, you might end up waiting so long you do nothing.

Getting clear on your real goals also helps when you're caught in a comparison trap. Psychology professor Sonja Lyubomirsky of UC Riverside ran a study where female college students were asked to solve anagrams. The students were told how they did compared to other participants. Unhappy students felt worse when they compared themselves to students who performed better than them, even if they did well themselves, whereas happy students weren't as fazed when comparing results. The advice here isn't to just "be happy" but instead, when you feel the urge to compare yourself to a friend or colleague that seems to have the perfect life (they don't), remember your own goals. Especially the ones you have control over. Knowing your own mission helps you stay focused.

Other people's lives are not meaningful reflections of how your own life is unfolding, so it's best to mind your business and keep it moving.

5. GAIN A NEW PERSPECTIVE.

Getting lost in thought can make our worlds very small. When I'm experiencing too much mental chatter, it feels like nothing else exists—and me and my problems take up all my attention. It's almost claustrophobic. That's why it's helpful to gain some perspective and remember that you are not your thoughts.

Let's turn back to the work of psychologist and neuroscientist Ethan Kross. One technique he suggests is what's known as temporal distancing, which essentially means creating some mental space. Let's say you're thinking about trying to buy a home. You're stressed because you see friends with partners being able to afford much more than you can as a single person and it's leading you down a mental path where you imagine yourself stuck in a too-small apartment for the rest of your life.

Okay, let's slow down here. If you catch yourself heading into a negative thought spiral, acknowledge that, and recognize that maybe it's not the best time to think about making a big financial decision. "There's absolutely zero benefit that will come right now from you thinking about it this way. Your executive functions are blasted. You have no capacity to do this right now," notes Kross.

Why not promise yourself you'll come back to the subject tomorrow or in a week? You might find that some time away from the thought allows you to see things more clearly. In this example, you might realize that renting still provides you a great place to live in a walkable neighborhood you love, mortgage interest rates are trash right now, and, hey, you can use the money you might have spent on roof repair for a fabulous trip.

You can also practice temporal distancing by mentally time traveling. Look to the past: Have there been other times you went through this problem? How did you get through it? You can mentally time travel into the future, too. Kross suggests asking yourself: How are you going to think about this in a week from now? A month from now? What about in five years? What about when you're dead? (That last one always humbles me.)

You can also do the old "talk to yourself like you would a friend" technique. Kross says the hack here is to use what's known as distanced self-talk. Tweak your language by using your own name. (*Meghan, you're not in love with that guy. You just need a nap.*) Using the third person can make us feel like we're getting outside council. It's effective because it's often easier to give someone guidance rather than to take your own advice.

It's also helpful to try to zoom out even further. Try to think of yourself as a literal fly on the wall, observing your situation. Kross and his colleagues have done studies on this very technique. Turns out, taking a distanced perspective, like that of a fly on a wall, led participants to feel better compared to those asked to recount an upsetting event from a first-person perspective.

Visualizing can also help. I sometimes imagine my ruminative thoughts as me playing hopscotch. Once I mentally hop all the way to square ten at the end of the line—say I realize I've reached the logical end of my catastrophic thinking—I visualize hopping backward on one leg back to square one, where I can regroup.

If you've got a highly visual mind's eye, you can take this further. In *Detox Your Thoughts,* clinical psychologist Andrea Bonior suggests imagining the color, texture, and temperature of your negative thoughts. Maybe they're storm clouds—for me, they are oily, purple ooze. Now with that physical embodiment in mind, she suggests visualizing clearing it away—the dark clouds fading to blue sky, the ooze melting away to reveal a clean surface. This practice helps further distance yourself from the thought.

I'd be remiss not to mention a classic—for a reason—tool: journaling. Journaling is not just dramatically recounting why you didn't want to go to the camp dance with that dude with the mole (it was a whole thing, I promise). It's also a helpful practice that leaves the rumination on the page and not in your mind. Psychologist James Pennebaker at the University of Texas at Austin has done groundbreaking work in what's known as expressive writing, or journaling about thoughts and feelings during an emotionally difficult time. He's done studies that showed expressive writing served as an emotional booster for depression-prone college students. So much of a booster, in fact, that the students who regularly journaled showed fewer depression symptoms after six months. To Pennebaker, expressive writing can help people better accept emotions while also giving new meaning to the story in their head. The key is to not judge yourself while writing. Although journaling on its own certainly has limits, it might lead to some surprising new insights.

I know some people find it too cringey to do, but this is what I like about going through my old journals. I'm confronted with a litany of concerns and worries about past romantic woes. But many times, I don't even remember writing those entries, much less the feelings described on the page. It's always a comfort to know that, hey, this random guy I dated for a month didn't actually break my heart. I got through it and never think about him anymore.

6. FIND THE "BIGGER, BETTER OFFER."

Anxious and ruminative thinking can be a bit like eating junk food. It might feel good in the moment, but too much of it will negatively impact us in the long run.

Maybe a so-so date revs up your thoughts and you start catastrophizing. *Why do I keep having these annoying time-suck dates? Is this the only kind of dating that's out there? God, is this the only kind of romance I'll ever experience?*

Do you feel more worked up after this mental bitch session? Do you feel sadder? Are you further away from calm? Yeah, this kind of thinking isn't ultimately rewarding. Brewer

recommends noticing how ruminating actually makes us feel, which in turn helps us become disenchanted with the behavior. The more you can recognize the anxious thinking for what it is—unhelpful and completely not fun—the less attractive it becomes to your brain.

It sounds too good to be true—just realize that ruminating feels bad and you won't want to do it as often? But it works because our brains operate on a reward-based learning system, says Brewer. When our brains experience something positive, we like it and seek it out. When we experience something negative, we dislike it and avoid it. What can we do instead when met with a potentially anxiety-provoking moment? Brewer recommends what he calls the "bigger, better offer"—one with the winning combination of curiosity and kindness.

Curiosity helps bring us to the present moment, which helps us better see that living in a tangle of rumination isn't as rewarding as we thought. When the worry trigger comes up (*When am I going to meet somebody?*), we can instead think:

- What am I looking forward to this week?
- Can I move my body?
- Can I do something creative right now?
- Who can I reach out to for connection?

Finding paths to more engaging, kinder activities are invitations to flip the question of "why am I so unhappy?" into "how can I live an engaged, rich life right in this moment?" In his research, Brewer found mindful curiosity not only leads to a more expansive mental state but quiets the posterior cingulate cortex, where the brain shows activity for cravings (like that mental junk food, rumination). That makes curiosity a more rewarding state than worry. Plus, it's an inherently kinder way to engage with yourself. A bigger, better offer.

Even with all I know about overthinking, it's still hard for me to give up the "why" of rumination. But the "why" doesn't always need to be investigated. "The 'why' is probably something that happened in the past," Brewer reminds me. "We can't change something that happened in the past, but we can change the future by how we behave both physically and mentally and how we think in the present moment."

As someone who's deeply therapized, I often feel the urge to rip open my emotional floorboards and see what's causing the rot. If you're feeling the same and feel a tad attached to those whys, let's ease into a better way to engage with them.

Investigating your identity, history, and trauma is an important part of life. But for many of us, it's not a useful daily practice. When the swirling thoughts creep in, you can acknowledge the hard things that are a part of your story, but you don't have to do deep self-analysis while you're just trying to get through your day. Try some of the tools from this chapter to quiet the unhelpful thoughts. Flip the "why" into a "what" and see what changes. Get a little mental distance. Give your brain a bigger, better offer. Doing the work is important, but so is knowing how and when it's helpful to process the root of a problem and when it's time to step away.

Our brains are marvelous learning machines that with practice will start to see more exits when the rumination creeps in. It can be slow going at first, but the shift is beautiful to experience. You might still find yourself going back to that old, negative story about yourself sometimes. But hopefully, with time, you'll be able to acknowledge that it's just a story, not reality. You can close that book for now.

ACTIVITY

- When you find yourself looping the same thought, journal for ten minutes about the topic you're ruminating about. Notice if you feel better after the journaling session.

- Identify what helps you get from the venting stage to the perspective stage. Ask a loved one for their help making that transition next time you need to vent.

PRACTICE

- Catch yourself when you start to ruminate. Think to yourself, "I notice that I'm starting to ruminate."

- Track your ruminations. Pinpoint what sets it off and note your behavior when it gets going.

- Convert "why me?" thoughts into "what can I do?" thoughts. What are three actionable steps you can take to help you move toward your goals?

- Practice temporal distancing. Are you going to care about this in a month? A year? Have you gotten through moments like this before?
- Try practicing curiosity when met with an anxiety trigger.

4

Building a Life You Love

WHEN I WAS A JUNIOR PRODUCER AT NPR, I'd walk into each shift praying for an easy day. I was temping on a broadcast news magazine where the goals were to be accurate, up-to-date, and punctual. All that is threatened by what's known as "crashing." If you are forced to work on your piece of the broadcast minutes or even seconds before it goes to air, you are crashing. Maybe there's breaking news and you need to track down an expert on Libyan politics or a reporter is having trouble uploading audio to the server and they are already behind schedule. Crashing is caused by anything that puts you behind schedule. The look of a producer crashing is distinct. Their eyes are locked on their computer. They get snippy at anyone trying to ask them questions. They are usually muttering curse words under their breath (or sometimes out loud). When you're crashing nothing feels as important at that moment as the piece you're trying to get to air on time. It's stressful.

While I was doing all I could to avoid crashing in my professional life, it was, unfortunately, my main mode when it came to dating. I threw myself completely into dating with intense focus. I tried to play the so-called numbers game by lining up date after date. This was my future happiness on the line, so I had to give it my all, right? That imaginary clock was ticking in my ear while I was sipping cocktails with yet another stranger from the internet. I dated like I was trying to meet a do-or-die deadline.

Then March 2020 rolled around, bringing a global coronavirus pandemic. Suddenly, I couldn't date with as much fervor when I was living with my mother in suburban Maryland and Cloroxing groceries. Sitting in the same place where I had done my homework for my high school AP Government class, I would read articles about how creative people were getting when it came to dating in quarantine.

These people waved at each other from their roofs every day and now they are dating! Tricks for nailing a FaceTime date! Seven tips to make your Zoom background more romantic!

I couldn't muster the drive to go into crashing mode. How were these people finding the energy to date during a global pandemic? There was lots of advice about how to do it even as the world was crumbling, but none of it felt realistic to me. Why were we pretending we could still date like we did before? I felt frustrated and stuck. One night while making dinner, I threw a plastic colander across the room in rage. It was embarrassing (not even a vase or a glass to shatter dramatically like in the movies?)—so many real horrors were happening, after all—but I fully snapped. I had thought if I just threw myself enough into dating—if I gave it the same focus as I did work—I would be rewarded. But crashing my dating life hadn't worked when I was going on multiple dates a week and it certainly wasn't working now. The pandemic showed me I had less control than I thought.

I had been approaching my dating life with what Professor Robert Vallerand at the Université du Québec à Montréal calls "obsessive passion." This state is the result of being too invested in an activity that feels attached to a person's identity and self. The pressure of obsessive passion feels uncomfortable because it's often connected to feelings of social acceptance or self-esteem.

According to Vallerand, "people with an obsessive passion can thus find themselves in the position of experiencing an uncontrollable urge to partake in the activity . . . The passion for the activity comes to control the person."

Sound familiar? I felt this in the relentlessness of modern dating, from "playing the numbers game" to always keeping one eye open for a potential partner. Sure, someone out there may find a partner through these means. But more often, dating-app obsessive passion leads to burnout. Vallerand notes in his study that obsessive passion can create negative emotional experiences (check) "while reducing the positive affective outcomes that would normally be experienced." Basically, obsessive passion is us getting in our own way.

A gentler approach is what Vallerand calls "harmonious passion." This is when you pursue something with your authentic self. People who engage in harmonious passion freely engage in an activity "without any or little contingencies attached to it." That sense of being controlled by the activity is nowhere to be found. Vallerand notes that this kind of passion "occupies a significant but not overpowering space in the person's identity and is in harmony with other aspects of the person's life" and results in "a flexibility and a mindful open manner that is conducive to positive experiences." Activities engaged in with harmonious passion are driven by our values and not by compulsion or desire for control.

In this chapter, we are going to step away from focusing on what a future partnered life might look like and instead build a life that makes us proud now. We lay the groundwork by learning to accept our current reality. Then we'll get clear about our values so we can live a life that feels more authentic to ourselves.

You have a gift when you are single—freedom. Singleness is a sacred place where you get to create your own safe haven in the present and future. As your own best partner, you can pursue what you really want, and need, and expect in life. What is it that drives you? What is it you want, above all else? While you might indeed want a romantic partner, for this exercise I'm going to ask you to take that idea off the table. Let's think about creating a life that feels good no matter our relationship status. How can you let go of obsessive passion for a romantic partner and instead bring a harmonious passion to your own life?

Accepting now

Let's start with getting clear about right now. First, we have to find acceptance in the reality of singlehood. It's difficult to cast a vision of a fulfilling single future if there is dissatisfaction about the single present.

Accepting singleness doesn't mean you have to "give up" the desire for a future romantic partner. There is room to both want a partner eventually and plan a meaningful life without one. Holding these two seemingly opposing desires side by side can help us move forward.

Dialectical behavioral therapy tools can be of use here. DBT helps us tolerate discomfort, live with more emotional skill so we can level with "the nature of reality," says Dr. Shireen Rizvi, professor of clinical psychology and director of the Dialectical Behavior Therapy Clinic at Rutgers University.

"It's based on this philosophy that attempts to explain the nature of reality, which is that there is always tension, there's always polarization, there's always going to be that conflict within ourselves and between ourselves," says Rizvi. Instead of fighting frustrations, DBT aims to help people accept (even at times love) them.

"There's always going to be that conflict within ourselves and between ourselves."

— Dr. Shireen Rizvi

Start with practicing acceptance. Rizvi says this practice is about shifting from a place of rejecting reality to accepting the facts. Suppressing frustration often leads to suffering. Acceptance is about acknowledging what is happening. If you're noticing some resistance to the idea that romantic partnership is not in the cards right now, it's unlikely you'll feel complete ease the first time you try practicing acceptance. It's not a one-and-done exercise. Rizvi told me acceptance is a lifelong practice. According to Rizvi, here's how to start practicing what's known as radical acceptance:

1. Start by noticing your resistance.
2. Check in with your body. How does it feel to resist?
3. Take a deep breath. Remind yourself that things are exactly how they are.

We might not like certain aspects of our realities, but this is how it is at this moment. Practicing radical acceptance doesn't mean accepting or approving of harmful or abusive situations, or giving up on something you'd like to change, it simply aims to help you see reality more clearly so you can move forward with wisdom. You might start to find that coming back to acceptance over and over again means letting go bit by bit of an idea of your life unfolding in one specific way. Radical acceptance is about "opening yourself to fully experiencing reality as it is in this one moment," writes psychologist Marsha Linehan, the founder of DBT.

There might be some grief that comes up in this process. Grief for a vision of a life you thought would look differently. Rizvi says if a patient came to her feeling this way, she'd remind them to treat themselves like they would a grieving friend. Hopefully with time, this self-compassion will soften the edges of your grief.

Ideally, radical acceptance leads to a growing sense of calm with your present moment. We can bolster that feeling by folding in additional skills to promote positive emotions as we enjoy our singlehood.

Learning the new ABCs

To set us up for success as we plan our single lives, we are going to learn some new ABCs. This is a classic DBT tool kit known as ABC PLEASE. The ABCs stand for tools that help reduce vulnerability to negative thoughts and feelings, and the PLEASE part is about daily self-care habits (resting when you're physically ill, eating well, avoiding mood-altering drugs, getting enough sleep and exercise) that promote general well-being. Let's dive in.

A: ACCUMULATING POSITIVES

"Accumulating positives is about doing something every day that gives you a sense of joy or pleasure," says Rizvi. These can be small acts like spending time with your pet, walking to get a coffee, or moving your body in a joyful way. It's very much the "I deserve a little treat" philosophy. The idea is that these everyday small pleasures help build up a reserve that buffers you against negative thoughts and events (within reason). Accumulating positives helps you feel day-to-day

enjoyment in your singlehood, but it can also help you with larger goals. Maybe you enjoy cartooning and making zines. You dream of writing a full-length graphic novel someday. You might accumulate positives by drawing a few times a week because it feels good, but that regular practice can also help bring you closer to your larger goal of writing that novel. And it helps with the next part of the ABCs . . .

B: BUILDING MASTERY

Doing things that not only give you pleasure but a sense of accomplishment is empowering. You don't need to be an expert to feel the benefits of building mastery. I know I'm far from being a ranked tennis player, but when I get a really good forehand hit in, damn, it feels nice.

Ask yourself: What's something I can do every day that makes me feel accomplished?

It could be a hobby but it could also be moving your body that day or paying a bill—anything that makes you feel accomplished counts says Rizvi. When you get that "cross it off your list" feeling from cleaning your room or scoring a goal for your rec soccer team, be mindful and appreciate it.

C: COPING AHEAD

Let's mentally time travel again. Imagine yourself in the future not just enjoying singlehood but *really* doing it with flair and ease. Are you traveling around the world with confidence? Happily raising a child? Starting a successful business? Maybe even just strolling through a park by yourself with a smile on your face? In DBT this technique of putting on an imaginary rehearsal is called coping ahead. It's imagining a potentially challenging future scenario and then visualizing yourself doing well in that moment. In the short term, it might be imagining you going home for the holidays and artfully deflecting your grandmother's questions about finding a husband. Look how much it doesn't bother future you! This practice is less about problem-solving and more about priming yourself with that feeling of "I got this."

Coping ahead helps reduce your vulnerability to getting overwhelmed in triggering scenarios. Rizvi suggests identifying how you could prepare for a challenging moment or what you might need to be successful in a given situation. Would living comfortably in singlehood mean having a solid support system? Does it mean prioritizing a creative practice? Or just feeling confident that your single life is a valid one?

The ABCs help your day to day feel more positive, and over time they build a mental bulwark against pesky negative thoughts and experiences about singlehood or anything else. Now that we're feeling more confident about our single reality, what's next?

Strengthening your foundation

You don't need to wait for a partner to participate in life. Let's get specific for a moment to focus on a few arenas in your life you can grow now.

If you are single and living on your own, life is already more expensive. The median wealth of married people under age thirty-five was nine times that for single women and three times that for single men, according to data from the

US Census in 2021. While the amount of never-married women in the labor market has grown, according to a 2023 report from Wells Fargo, they still make only 92.1 percent of what never-married men make—down from 95.8 percent just a decade earlier. In a survey of a thousand people by *Forbes*, one in three singles say they have stayed in a relationship longer than they otherwise would have because of its financial benefits. Although marriage isn't guaranteed to result in happiness, it can lead to more wealth.

"I would say to folks who feel discouraged . . . you're not wrong in your frustration," Berna Anat, financial educator and hype woman, and author of the book *Money Out Loud: All the Financial Stuff No One Taught Us*, told me. So many of life's financial milestones and institutions are structured around partnership, Anat says. It's not all bad news: Single women own more homes than single men. A single person has complete control over their finances so they're not on the hook for a spouse's poor financial decisions. But still, Anat (who identifies as "aggressively single") says it's okay to feel irritated about how "structurally and morally backwards" it is for our financial institutions to favor couples. After that justifiable feeling, though, focus on what she calls "financial wholeness." Part of that is understanding the basics of budgeting, saving, getting out of debt, and so on, "but it's also getting right with your financial emotional history" so you can make goals for future you. That means understanding what in your personal history triggers certain reactions around money and then making a plan for yourself. Maybe you find it hard to save for an emergency fund because you shop online when you're stressed. In this case, setting up an automated transfer to your savings could be the solution.

As a single person, you get to shape your life with money as a tool. When it comes to retirement, Anat suggests you save early and save aggressively. Mess around with a retirement calculator to get "spreadsheet Virgo-level clear" on how much you can afford to save for retirement from each paycheck and map out your next decades. As a child-free single woman, Anat says she wants to be set up for down the road—but she also wants to budget wisely so she can enjoy her life now.

And while it might feel morbid, you'll want to create a will. A living will clarifies your medical wishes, and a simple will can direct the distribution of your assets after death. Although Anat lists her nieces as her beneficiaries, she says that might not be the right call for everyone. You might want your assets to go to a cause you support or to a friend. "Your money doesn't actually need to mother anybody," says Anat.

You also don't have to do this planning alone. You could hire a certified public accountant once a year to help with your taxes. Anat always takes advantage of that annual appointment to ask her accountant any non-tax-related finance questions. And I would be remiss if I didn't plug my podcast, *Life Kit*, as a great free resource for friendly financial advice to get you up to speed.

It's a good idea to get right with your money now because it'll serve you the rest of your life—no matter how it turns out.

Taking up hobbies

In the competitive culture of where I grew up in Montgomery County, Maryland, you knew where you stood. You weren't *really* an athlete unless you were on a varsity sports team and in the travel league. *Real* theater kids auditioned for every school production each year. The best art nerds had their work on display in the hallways. Even though I grew up playing tennis, I stayed in my extracurricular lane (which is why I can say I've been a villager in *Fiddler on the Roof*, a Who in *Seussical*, and a brassy cab driver in *On the Town*). Once I was in my twenties and free of the social constraints of high school, I went back to sports without the pressure. I picked up tennis again. I joined a volleyball league that played in sand courts overlooking the Lincoln Memorial. During a game one of my teammates turned to me and said something I'd never heard before: "You're an athlete." I wasn't amazing, but I was there and having fun. By that point in my life I didn't need the validation of the label, but it was fun to stumble into it.

This is all to say: Don't let preconceived notions of yourself hinder you from trying something you might enjoy. Hobbies help us experience flow and play. They lead to better mood, lower heart rate, and less stress. If you're hoping to pick up a new hobby or get back into an old one, here are a few approaches to try:

1. If you already have a hobby you love, make time for it. Schedule "building miniatures" or "weekly running group" in your calendar and honor that time.

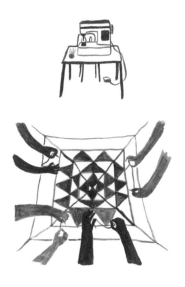

2. Try having a solo hobby and a group hobby. Making your own clothes might mean focusing over a sewing machine by yourself for hours, but also try a monthly meetup for vintage lovers. That way, you can practice your skill on your own time and also share your passion with like-minded others.

3. Find identity-based communities within your hobby of choice. Whether for you that means joining a queer birding group or a woman of color running group, identity-based groups can feel safer to explore and even more enjoyable.

4. Try a hobby you've always wanted to do but never had the time for. Maybe it's a beginners' class in pottery or a community environmentalist walk. Commit to trying a few interests and then see which once makes you feel the most alive.

5. Remove any pressure to be good at the hobby. You're never going to be a master on the first try. Ask others for help. Seek inspiration.

Pets

Don't wait for a partner to experience the love of a pet. If you've got a dog, cat, lizard, or bird-sized hole in your heart and you have the means to take care of one, go for it. Pets foster a sense of belonging and connection. Researchers have found that cortisol levels drop when people spend time with dogs for even just five minutes. I got my dog, Margo, in the summer of 2020. I was tired of waiting for a guy to show up to do dog ownership with me. The first time she sat in my lap, I cried. I had a lot of unconditional love to give and wanted to direct it somewhere. A pet was a wonderful way to do just that.

It wasn't easy to raise a puppy on my own, but I was never really alone. I had friends and family that gave me advice over text, sent me YouTube videos of puppy-training techniques, and brought over toys bigger than my 2.5-pound puppy's entire body. Margo and I learned together. She is there when people disappoint me, ready to radiate the love I've invested into her right back at me.

Engaging your senses

It's frustrating to not experience touch as frequently as you might desire. Not to mention that finding a partner—even a casual partner who makes you feel safe and respected—takes a lot of energy. My advice: Widen the lens of touch and sensuality for yourself. There are lots of ways to be dropped into your body and experience pleasure that don't involve partners.

In her book *Pleasure Activism: The Politics of Feeling Good*, adrienne maree brown reminds us that "pleasure is a measure of freedom." She practices what she calls pleasure activism, which is the idea that "we all need and deserve pleasure and that our social structures must reflect this." In a world where marginalized people are discouraged, punished, even killed for seeking pleasure, brown believes it's a defiant act to "prioritize the pleasure of those most impacted by oppression." To feel good in a society that says you shouldn't is an act of protest.

"Pleasure is a measure of freedom."

— adrienne maree brown

Pleasure can mean orgasm, sure, but it also means all the ways you can feel delight and aliveness in your body. "I like to smell good, taste everything yummy, feel how alive skin is, listen to sounds of breath and pleasure, see the beauty of flesh and bones. Laugh uncontrollably. Play. Feel alive," brown writes.

Pay attention to what gives you pleasure in your body, brown says, and it will give way to growth. Maybe that's making sure your bed has wonderful sheets, stretching your muscles deeply, feeling the breeze coming off a body of water, sweating on a hike, applying lotion, sunbathing (with sunscreen), or dancing.

This pairs well with another pleasure framework: sensualism. It's a framework from philosophy professor Céline Leboeuf of Florida International University. In one essay, Leboeuf examines how the philosopher Simone de Beauvoir took pleasure in her frequent hikes. She loved the rigor of hiking and driving her body to "the very limit of its endurance." This practice was of particular note because de Beauvoir, as a feminist philosopher, was keenly aware of her body's relationship to herself in a society that sees women as primarily sexual objects. Leboeuf theorized that hiking gave de Beauvoir this feeling of sensualism, a path that offers a "different way of living the body."

By the way, you can, in this quest to diversify sensuality, also include the most literal form of it: sexual pleasure. Buy the sex toy. Have an orgasm. Have sex when it feels right to you.

I know that partnered sex can provide more than an orgasm. The component of touch from another person can feel irreplaceable. But we can also broaden our scope of safe touch beyond sex. Cuddling (with consent) with friends. Getting massages. Even self-touch on the scalp, neck, arms, or legs any time or before masturbation can feel soothing. You deserve pleasure, so seek it out.

Building your support network

When you're single, it's fun to get to pick the paint for your apartment with no need to compromise on your color of choice. It's less fun to paint it all by yourself or to have to pay painters with just your credit card. The admin of adulthood can sometimes feel overwhelming alone. A partner *might* make household tasks easier—if you're lucky. But research shows that in heterosexual couples, women are still doing the majority of the housework even when they're working a paying job. So maybe we all need help.

Singles still need support with day-to-day tasks. Even if you are hyper-independent, getting a little help can better set you up for success. The way to do that is to seek out lots of different, specific pockets of support.

I should note that this is not encouraging you to see everyone in your life as a resource only. It's simply about making an appropriate ask from people who care about you.

- Who do you already know?
- What kind of expertise do they have?
- What level of ask can you make?
- What can you help them with to reciprocate support?

Looking ahead to a single future

I have never been able to answer the question "Where do you want to be in five years?" I know it's a way to ask about goals, but even as a driven person, I find it hard to pinpoint a concise list. (Be healthy? Have a career I'm proud of? Oh god, do these need to be more specific?!) I didn't even know I wanted to write a book until my lovely and talented collaborator suggested it to me (thanks, LA!). Besides, life changes so quickly, how can anyone come up with definite goals?

As we work on what our future might look like as a single person, it's tempting to be strictly focused on goals. Goals are great, but there might be a better way to engineer a life that feels good to us.

First, let's dig into why goals aren't always great North Stars. In her book *Real Self-Care: A Transformative Program for Redefining Wellness (Crystals, Cleanses, and Bubble Baths Not Included)*, Dr. Pooja Lakshmin writes that people make random goals all the time but "rarely do we identify the values underneath them." That's because, she told me, we often conflate values and goals. Goals provide structure and actions, but "values are qualities that we embody when we're moving toward a specific outcome," Lakshmin told me. To her, "goals are the things that you do, values are the way you do them."

"Goals are the things that you do, values are the way you do them."

— Dr. Pooja Lakshmin

This distinction was a revelation to me—it relieved the pass/fail pressure I often felt about my goals. (Didn't make it to every national park? You're human.) Plus, Lakshmin notes, being overly focused on reaching a specific goal means there's likely a label we've projected onto it. A romantic relationship unfairly gets the label of happiness, wholeness, or moral goodness. Chasing a label means being more focused on what others and society want from you, not what you want for yourself.

"You can get hyper-fixated on these goals and mistake the goals for happiness," Lakshmin told me. "The thing that brings fulfillment is being connected to your values." And those values are individual to you.

This approach is a good gut check. Is your heart really set on freezing your eggs or taking on a mortgage by yourself because it honors your values? Or are you doing something because you feel like you need to check it off a predetermined list?

One way to better understand how to balance your goals and values is to ask yourself what, how, and why. Lakshmin suggests the following exercise in *Real Self-Care*. Pick a goal (what), identify the value beneath that goal that you want to embody (how), and then clarify what she calls a personal manifesto (why). This might look like:

- What: Become mentor to young women.
- How: I value generosity and sharing knowledge.
- Why: Because I don't think I want my own kids but I want to support the next generation in my community.

After this exercise we can layer on the practice of accumulating positives. What's something you could do each day to feel like you're living in your values and by doing so, moving closer to a goal?

Nothing here is set in stone, by the way. "It's completely normal for values to change over the course of your life," says Lakshmin. Values can change for many reasons—experience, your stage of life, the state of the world. Allowing for flexibility helps make your choices feel more authentic to you.

Staying in relationship with your values

Close your eyes. Think about a moment when you felt really great and alive and now visualize it. What comes to mind? What is it about this moment that feels valuable? What made it feel like a worthwhile experience? This exercise was posed to me by Meghan Watson, a psychotherapist and owner of Bloom Psychology & Wellness, a therapy collective in Toronto. The moment that immediately came to me was a New Year's Eve dinner party my best friend, Caitlin, threw with her husband. The seemingly endless dinner table had lots of friends around it, passing pasta and wine back and forth between candles, and the conversation was free-flowing and warm. That snapshot tells me something about my values—I love being around the people I love, who are kind and generous. I love celebrating. And I love pasta.

There are lots of different theories on values, but the idea behind many of them is that leading a values-driven life helps us flourish. But what does it mean to flourish? I turned to Kelly Crace, a psychologist and associate vice president for health and wellness at the College of William & Mary, whose thirty-five-year research career has been dedicated to understanding what really promotes flourishing. "We discovered that values were a really important part of the notion of flourishing. But in a way that was surprising to us," he told me.

Crace says there's a misconception about how values

work—that is, the more time and attention you put toward your values, the more effective you'll be at expressing them. In Crace's work, he's found that there isn't an upward linear relationship between values and attention. "What we actually found is it's more of a curvilinear relationship," says Crace. Once we care about something, pressure and risk get automatically added into the equation. Uncertainty, doubt, and loss are on the table. Often, people cope with fear through perfectionism or procrastination. If you value achievement, for example, and become laser focused on a prestigious award or getting married, you're too attached to a result rather than the value itself and all the other ways you could be embodying it. If putting too much pressure and attention on our values can backfire, what's a better mindset?

"Values [are] a really important part of the notion of flourishing."
— Kelly Crace

It's all about having an intentional, healthy relationship with them, about finding a sweet spot between acknowledging their importance and not letting an outcome become the key. That means focusing less on pursuing happiness and more on striving for purpose. Essentially, placing more attention on *expressing* your values day to day.

Try asking yourself "What can I do to act on my values today?" When life throws you difficulties, a truly flourishing person asks themselves, "How do I still healthfully engage in things that matter to me?" According to Crace, a flourishing person who had a bad day will say to themselves, "I succeeded; I did what mattered to me. The world just kind of beat me up for it today," says Crace. This approach means rooting into your values and being flexible instead of letting external factors or heated emotions take over.

How do we identify our values? Crace and his colleagues developed the Life Values Inventory, a free online quiz to give you a snapshot of your current values. I encourage you to do the full quiz since it's very thorough, but here are the key questions:

1. What values matter to you right now?
2. Of those values, what matters most to you? How would you rank them?
3. How often do those values guide your behavior?

I like these questions because they prompt you to be honest with yourself. When confronted with a wall of values, it's easy to think, *Well, all those are important to me!* But thinking about which ones drive your day-to-day behavior helps sort out which ones are the most in play for you at this time in your life. Here are some of the values Crace uses in his work to get you started—feel free to add your own:

- Responsibility
- Health and activity
- Belonging
- Independence
- Achievement
- Concern for others
- Interdependence
- Objective analysis
- Privacy
- Creativity
- Concern for environment
- Financial prosperity
- Humility
- Spirituality

The official quiz will have you rate how frequently your actions are guided by each value. Take note of the values that rise to the top. Now it's time to understand your current relationship to these values. Place your top values into these categories developed by Crace:

- High priority
- Over-attention
- Under-attention
- Medium/low

"The most common reaction around real deep values work is a combination of confirmation and affirmation, frustration and sorrow," Crace told me. I felt all those things. For me, I put responsibility, health, belonging, and interdependence in the high-priority category. I feel good about how I show up for my friends and make nourishing meals (interdependence, health and activity), but then the value of responsibility can veer into unhealthy territory when combined with concern for others lurking in my over-attention column (see: people-pleasing habit). In my under-attention column, I put objective analysis, privacy, and creativity. That tells me I could stand to prioritize quiet time to practice my creative writing more often.

Crace also suggests looking at this breakdown and asking yourself what value is currently bringing you the most fulfillment? The most stress? What value do you hope to affect the most in the next year? If you could only be remembered for three values, what would they be?

For the day-to-day practice embodying your values, Crace suggests asking yourself a few questions:

1. What matters today?
2. Of those things, what matters most?
3. What can I give with what I have today?

Maybe you want to honor your value of concern for the environment, so on a day with lots of free time you attend a community cleanup. Or perhaps on a meeting-heavy workday you spend a few moments appreciating the birds outside your office window. Both actions are examples of living in your values. For me, this paradigm of meeting your values where *you* are that day relieves a lot of pressure.

Crace suggests taking a moment at the end of the day to appreciate how you were able to step into your values. Think about what went well and what you could do to prepare for the next day. Remember, flourishing isn't about being perfect; it's about authentically embodying your values in the ways that make the most sense for your life.

Planning for the future

If we've made it this far, we've done the work to accept our reality and even like it. We've shifted our mindset from chasing goals to embodying values. Now it's time to plan! The good and bad news about singlehood is that you get to make all the decisions. Where to live, whether to have kids, how

to spend your money—it's all up to you. When faced with a difficult choice, it's not always clear what to do.

Do you listen to your emotions? Or your reason?

"Most of the time—and this is true in all of my clinical practice and supervision—people almost always say 'I want to be in reasonable mind. I want to get rid of emotions,'" says Shireen Rizvi. In DBT, there is a conceptual framework of the emotion mind and the reasonable mind. While it's tempting to strive to always operate from a place of reasonable mind, it's not always in our best interest. "If we're in reasonable mind and we have no emotions, we're actually losing a lot. We don't have values, we don't have compassion or empathy because those are informed by emotional experiences," says Rizvi. Excluding emotions leaves out a lot of important information and it can lead to finding less meaning in an experience. Not to mention that devaluing emotions and striving to always be solely rational is quite the patriarchal goal.

Swinging the pendulum too far in the other direction into a solely emotional mind isn't much help, either. That's when our emotions like sadness, anger, or shame can take over and dictate our actions.

Instead, the aim is to integrate both the emotion and reasonable minds to operate from what's known as a wise mind. The wise mind has roots in Buddhism, but for these purposes I'm drawing from the DBT skill framework. According to Rizvi, experiencing a wise mind feels almost like an "aha" moment. "It is often accompanied by a feeling of centeredness, a feeling of relief," she says. A wise mind takes into consideration both emotions and reason and then can take intentional action.

How do we tap into that wise mind? One option is to give yourself a pause before taking action. Sometimes letting time pass and coming back to a problem is the wise thing to do. Another strategy is to be aware when you are pulled too far into either emotion or reasonable mind. Once you find that awareness and take a pause, you can ask yourself a few questions:

- What does a wise mind think of this?
- What are my emotions telling me to do here?
- What is a reasonable mind telling me to do here?
- What is the wise thing to do here?

Don't try to force an answer. See what naturally arises. Remember: A wise mind is not about favoring emotions or reason. It's about having them come together harmoniously. Also, there's no need to come up with a future plan and stick to it indefinitely. Be open to change. Signs and opportunities in life don't always announce themselves in flashy neon. If you need to readjust and it still feels good, go for it.

Some big questions that can come up in singlehood can benefit from consideration with the wise mind:

- Could I be open to nonmonogamy?
- Do I want to consider a move farther from my support system?
- Could I be a single parent by choice?

These questions can feel like big forks in the road and some have limited time to answer. Instead of thinking of one path as right and another wrong, Crace says to conceive of a possibility of "two rights." Having a kid on your own is just as valid a version of a life as being child-free. But if you're already waffling, the idea of endless right choices may be more stress-inducing.

Here's an exercise Crace uses to narrow it down:

1. Write down one possible outcome of a decision.

2. Brainstorm all the factors that would move you toward that decision.

3. Brainstorm all the restrictive factors that would pull you away from that path.

4. Rate each factor from most important to you right now to least important.

5. Lastly, rate how reality-based each factor is. (Example: You think your parents will be disappointed if you become a single parent. Is that a valid worry based in reality? Or are they more likely to be excited to be grandparents?)

What this exercise does is illuminate the salience of your true core values. It also clarifies fears—what is actually a legitimate concern versus an unfounded anxiety?

Big decisions aren't usually made in one afternoon. They can happen over time. Pooja Lakshmin suggests taking a small step in one direction to test out how you feel. Perhaps a trial run of working abroad for a month or attending an informational session about egg freezing. Test, evaluate, and then reevaluate. She also recommends thinking back to other moments in your life when you made a big decision. How did you navigate it? What helped you make the final call?

This won't give you an instant, foolproof result (wouldn't that be nice), but this process will reveal what's really important to you. Remember, Lakshmin says, when you are staring down a hard choice, "the relationship isn't going to save you. The baby isn't going to save you. The only thing that will make you feel better and have the life you want actually is you."

It's difficult to be 100 percent sure about a hard decision. Your task is not to be completely settled. It is to figure out what is right enough for you. It all comes back to accepting what you have chosen and dealing with the reality of the situation. Even when you do make a big life choice, surprises will pop up and the plan might need to change again. You will need to continue to practice flexibility, acceptance, and self-knowledge about what values matter most to you. It all comes down to this: Who do you want to be?

ACTIVITY

JOURNAL PROMPTS:

- What would it take to feel good about a life without a romantic partner?

- What is it about a potential relationship that you think will make you happier? What do you *actually* need? What's been impeding you from meeting those needs?

- Think about what values motivate your behavior. Which ones do you prioritize? Which values do you want to bring more into your life?

- When facing a hard life decision, think about the peaks and valleys of your life so far. Are there any common themes? What lessons did you learn? What values did you embody in both the good and bad times that you feel proud of?

- Make a list of ways to accumulate positives. What are three things you could plan to do every day that build you up?

PRACTICE

- When you feel emotional resistance, practice acceptance before taking action.

- When you have a bad day, think if you were still able to honor your values in some way. What can you do differently tomorrow?

- Seek out pleasure—whether that's with movement, laughter, or touch.

- Appreciate the moments when you have stepped into your values.

5

Managing Emotions and Being Okay (Even When You Are Not)

"MOM?" I CROAK OUT. I'M SITTING ON THE couch wrapped up in blankets. My hand covers my face as if I'm trying to avoid being recognized. Even though I'm on the phone, I feel embarrassed by my tears.

I often make these calls to my mom when my emotions feel overwhelming—when I'm pacing around my apartment too much, when my body is buzzing with anger or sadness. When I can't see the path out, I call her.

"I'm just feeling so sad."

My mom has received a million calls like this. She snaps into Go Mode: "What happened?" We have a relationship where we talk almost every day. Although frequent, our talks are usually light chats about the day's to-do list, the frustration of rescheduling a doctor's appointment, or a quick laugh about something funny my aunt told her. But sometimes, we'll get into my dating life.

I hardly ever tell my friends about my first dates. And most of the time, there's nothing to tell. I hate the whole production. Many first dates feel like going up the first ascent of a roller coaster, but instead of teetering over the edge of the initial peak and feeling a thrill of the ride, we stop short. The car clicks backward back to the beginning of the track, dropping this disappointed rider off where we started.

"Well, I went on three dates with this guy, and, Mom, I really liked him."

"What did he do? What happened?" My mom wants to know the damage as soon as possible.

"I thought things were good, but then he just texted that he's not interested anymore"—my voice cracks—"and I feel like shit."

My mom almost always replies the same way: "What is wrong with these people?"

It helps to let out the emotions, but the familiar routine of this particular conversation feels bleak. Here I was again, playing out the same scenario, the two of us hitting the same marks with the same script. It makes my heart ache even more—the sadness feels permanent.

"I'm going to feel this way forever, aren't I?"

The short answer: No, I'm not. Even though it can feel that way, I'm not, and neither are you. It's easy to think of big, uncomfortable feelings like an invading force, an unpredictable enemy that descends upon you and wreaks havoc on your life. But even when it feels impossible to remember, it's helpful to know that emotions are actually

"The more that we can be intentional about our choice and feel good about it, the more confidence we will feel about our decisions."
— Dr. I-Ching Grace Hung

more like messengers with useful information. You can engage them, partner up. There are ways to key into our emotions and listen to what they have to say instead of letting them overwhelm you.

When it comes to emotions, "we often think good or bad," psychologist I-Ching Grace Hung told me. But if, instead of judging emotions as positive or negative, we can think of them as neutral data, "that becomes a whole different game."

We've learned how to tame our anxious thoughts; now let's move from the head to the heart. In this chapter, we'll go over tools for managing emotions. You'll find that these complement what we've already learned about combating negative thinking so we're not starting from scratch. These tools can't ensure permanent happiness, but that's not the goal anyway. Turbulent times happen and emotions will inevitably arise. And I want to be clear that there are very real reasons to be angry and sad in this world, and while there are techniques to manage what is in your control, there are also potential factors like chemical imbalances and mood disorders that are not. The practices that follow can help in managing emotions, but they are not meant to be substitutes for professional medical help.

We may be tempted to return to unhelpful thoughts like the *only* way we can be happy is in a relationship with someone else. But even in the happiest relationships, you can't exactly escape yourself (believe me, I've tried). Everyone can benefit from being able to emotionally regulate themselves from a place of acceptance and self-compassion. There is a more profound love on the other side.

A different way of looking at emotions

Before exploring tools for managing them, let's dive a little deeper into emotions themselves. Some ancient philosophers and physicians conceived of the mind as divided up into different regions, including a region specifically for emotions. This thinking laid the groundwork for the classical view of emotions. For example, in this framework, a person who experiences a certain stimulus—let's say someone cutting their chariot off in traffic—will then experience a supposedly distinct, universal emotion in response, in this case, anger.

Centuries later, there's been a provocative reimagining of this model, one that I find profoundly more nuanced and helpful. It was first outlined in 2017 by psychologist and neuroscientist Lisa Feldman Barrett. Barrett's lab reviewed over two decades of brain-imaging studies examining basic emotions. They found that no singular brain region was responsible for any specific emotion. In a telling example, her team found insufficient evidence to show that the amygdala, popularly associated with "fear" in the brain, always fires when fear is actually activated.

Barrett's model proposes what she calls the theory of constructed emotion. She suggests emotions aren't reactions, but constructions. Our bodies and minds respond to two main categories of sensations through what's known as interoception—one lever that feels pleasantness and unpleasantness and another lever that feels arousal or calm. Because our brains are predictive organisms, it takes in those sensations and responds by making some guesses about how to feel.

Here's how Barrett suggests an emotion is constructed with those two basic stimuli or levers. Let's say you've been ghosted by the last few people you dated. First of all, that's super annoying and they should have had the decency to at least text you that they were no longer interested. But based

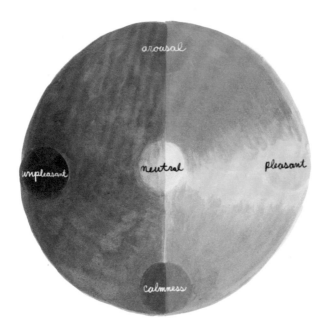

on those experiences, your brain is going to notice that recent pattern. Say you then go on a somewhat promising date. They make you laugh and you feel a little electricity when you lock eyes. But they haven't responded since your "I had a great time—let's do it again soon" text. And now your body is pulling those levers toward "unpleasant" and "high arousal." Your brain sees those signals go off and flips through its catalog of past experiences. "Remember these other people who ghosted? It's time to feel fear!"

Your emotional reaction of fear is a result of your brain making sense of this experience based on what it learned from your previous negative ones. That fear is unique to you, created by *your* brain as a response to *your* experiences. It is a construction that is highly personal and customized, according to Barrett's theory.

Here's where it gets good. This view of emotions as being constructed rather than inevitable means you have some *control* over them. I know it doesn't always feel that way. But Barrett suggests we can change by creating new experiences to alter how our brains construct our emotions. We are not just reacting machines. We can be collaborators with our emotions.

What emotional regulation really means

Emotional regulation does not mean eternal zen—that's unrealistic. It's perfectly possible to be angry and emotionally regulated or sad and emotionally regulated. "Emotional regulation is not maintaining calm, it's maintaining choice," says Britt Frank, licensed specialist clinical social worker and author of *The Science of Stuck: Breaking Through Inertia to Find Your Path Forward*. You can still access the logical part of your brain while feeling emotions. You're able to pick your words carefully and choose your actions wisely.

Emotional dysregulation, on the other hand, is when you become overwhelmed by emotion. When you're in this state, you're often unwilling to accept an emotion you're experiencing; sometimes you can't even recognize it. When you're emotionally dysregulated, it's harder to self-soothe and make rational decisions. "That's when we act out with impulsive behavior or compulsive actions or addictions," says Frank.

Perhaps you've been interrogated about your dating life for the hundredth time by a parent who clearly wants grandchildren. This time it's getting to you. You're fuming after the visit. Emotionally regulating in this situation would mean thinking about what's in your control and making decisions based on this knowledge. Perhaps you decide you will set boundaries with that parent next time you come over for dinner—a quick "the topic of dating is off-limits for me right now." Or maybe you decide to take a longer walk home to keep your body moving or wind down afterward with a movie that makes you laugh.

"Emotional regulation is not maintaining calm, it's maintaining choice."
— Britt Frank

Emotional dysregulation, however, looks like flying off the handle when the conversation stresses you, or storming off in a huff. In both situations, you're feeling the emotion. But with emotional regulation you're able to *manage* the feeling.

I should note, we're not grading on perfection here. No one can be expected to behave flawlessly every single time we have a big feeling. Sometimes we need big feelings to protect us. There may be outside factors beyond our control or we may be in an unsafe environment. If you're in an abusive relationship, a toxic workplace, or any other situation where you're in physical or emotional danger, emotional dysregulation is your body telling you it's time to get out.

Hopefully, this isn't your situation and your stresses are the more manageable kind. Everyday emotional regulation is acting with the knowledge that you have the ability to make choices about how you respond to your emotions when they arise.

How to embrace mindfulness (even if you really don't want to)

I know mindfulness gets recommended for just about everything. Feeling stressed at work? Mindfulness! Existential dread? Mindfulness! Can't pick what you want to wear for the day? Have you tried mindfulness?

Before taking up my own mindfulness practice, I was highly skeptical. I found it patronizing to be reminded to "stay in the moment." As if dealing with feelings could be that easy. After my first big breakup in my twenties, my emotions felt very heavy and overwhelming. I had backed myself into an emotional corner with my shame about being single. Despite my misgivings, I gave mindfulness a try because I felt like I was running out of options. And, I somewhat begrudgingly report, little by little, I started to notice more ease in my life. There wasn't some huge change like I was happy all the time, but I found myself a little more balanced. I didn't take criticism at work as personally, and the sting of romantic rejection was a little more tolerable. I felt able to stand up and walk away from that scary corner.

If you're skeptical of mindfulness, that's okay. I'm not prescribing long sessions of meditation (unless you want to!). Here's the thing about mindfulness, though: There's plenty of research to back up the benefits and it's free. You don't have much to lose here. Take it from a former skeptic—this shit works.

Mindfulness is powerful. Some mindfulness techniques can help with managing anxiety, depression, and stress. It helps people sleep better. Mindfulness is also useful for pain management for people dealing with chronic illnesses. And it can help you cope with negative emotions around single-ness, too.

So, what exactly is mindfulness? Essentially, mindfulness is purposefully paying attention to the present moment without judgment. That's the definition used by the mindfulness-based stress reduction program created by Dr. Jon Kabat-Zinn at the University of Massachusetts Memorial Health Center for Mindfulness. By being aware of the present moment, you're better able to slow down emotional reactivity.

While the concept of mindfulness is incredibly simple, practicing it can take some work. "The present moment is not something that's going to just happen by accident," says Kessonga Giscombé, a mindfulness and meditation teacher at Headspace. "[Being in the present moment is] going to take some intention and it's going to take some deliberateness."

Mindfulness is not necessarily about emptying your mind of thoughts, "it's bringing your full attention to whatever it is you're doing right here or now," says Giscombé. The beauty of mindfulness is that you can apply it to any and every activity. You can mindfully brush your teeth (*this toothbrush is moving across my lower set of teeth*), mindfully get dressed (*this sweater is fuzzy*), mindfully eat (*this chocolate bar tastes salty and sweet*).

As I mentioned earlier, I'm a super ruminator. It's really easy for me to get many trains of thought going at the same time, even while holding a conversation. I'll be engaged in talking to someone as my brain shouts out

"*If you want things to shift, you have to first accept [them].*"

— Kessonga Giscombé

items to add to my grocery list and rehearses scripts for how to tell a different friend I can't make their birthday party. It's loud in there. It's not helpful, nor is it considerate of the person I'm currently interacting with. To be mindful in that moment means to deliberately quiet down my thoughts and pay attention to what I'm doing.

After my breakups, I became quite attached to ruminating on my past hurts, admiring them all like they were treasures in a jewelry box. I felt like I didn't have time to be in the moment—look at all these old emotions I needed to deal with! But this obsessing over the past became exhausting. If you're always looking back over your shoulder, you're going to keep stumbling over what's right in front of you.

Before taking up this practice, I was worried I was too much of an emotional wreck for mindfulness to work for me. (Clearly, some self-judgment there.) Thankfully, Giscombé says you don't need to feel like you've got your life together to practice mindfulness. There's this idea, he says, that "if you practice mindfulness, you don't get angry. You're not jealous. You don't feel anxiety. You're always calm. It's just a huge misconception."

I can personally attest to the fact that it's fully possible to be a jealous bitch who also practices and benefits from mindfulness.

For psychologist I-Ching Grace Hung, who integrates Buddhist philosophy with Western psychology, mindfulness has the most utility when we can gain a little distance from our own perspective. Think of your perspective as a pair of glasses. In this example, they're glasses that might need a little cleaning. Smudges obscure your field of vision; scratches distort things on one side. Our lenses filter what we see and, in turn, what we see feels like reality. When we practice mindfulness, Hung says, "what we're doing is we're actually removing that lens as much as we can." Focusing on present moments of mindfulness is like peering over those cloudy glasses and seeing what's in front of us more clearly.

If you're looking to increase your mindfulness, sitting for meditation does help. Formal sit-down meditations are like jam sessions for your brain, says Hung. You're building the muscle of mindfulness. Giscombé advises his students to start small. When he was starting to meditate, he did only about three minutes a day. Three minutes became five minutes which became ten minutes and so on. Giscombé told me he started to notice an organic shift in how he moved through his days. "I was paying more attention to the things that I was doing and noticed that I wasn't as reactive."

Doesn't that sound nice?

Whether you meditate daily or practice some other mindfulness techniques, I have a feeling you'll notice a similar shift when it comes to your emotions. When I started my mindfulness practice, I realized I was able to take the emotional off ramp away from dysregulation more often. As Giscombé told me, mindfulness isn't just a practice, it's really a way of being.

When emotions feel *really* big

Whenever I walk my dachshund, Margo, I'm always on the lookout. For one, she is only about nine pounds so I'm making sure she doesn't get stepped on. But mostly, I'm looking out for her Little Dog Syndrome triggers. Believing herself to be more Doberman than tiny wiener dog, Margo tends to yap at most dogs that are bigger than her. My apologies to my neighbor and his Samoyed, Margo's inexplicable nemesis.

When Margo gets in this mood, she lunges forward and barks aggressively. She transforms from a sweet Beanie Baby–looking animal to a true terror in seconds. Because I know her triggers (big, fluffy all-white dogs, for one) I try my best to distract her when I see one coming. I tell her "front!" which is her signal to turn toward me, sit, and make eye contact. Typically, a little treat helps with this. On her best days, she snaps into focus, calmly makes eye contact with me, and lets the fluff ball dogs prance on by. But sometimes I don't catch her in time or sometimes she's having a bad day and then I'm

dragging her away with an apologetic smile at the other dog's owner.

Sometimes big emotional triggers will find us even when we try to avoid them, and it's hard to do anything when you're overwhelmed. The trick is to de-escalate when you're in that moment of heightened, blinding emotion. What we want to do when we're riled up (take note, Margo) is get back into our bodies. I know there's nothing worse than being told to take a deep breath when emotions are running high—but it really is helpful to turn the tension down a tad. When we're emotionally dysregulated, our prefrontal cortex, the rational thinking part of our brain, is offline. Trying to think your way out of an emotion is likely going to be counterproductive when you're really in your feelings.

Here are some tips to dial down the intensity and get back into the present moment, even when your brain isn't being helpful:

1. **Engage your five senses.** Pause and start to notice what's around you. List out the objects you see (*leafy tree, tiny blue flower, half-empty coffee cup*). Notice what you can feel (*fleece jacket, dog fur, fuzzy socks*). Do the same for what you can hear, smell, and taste. This is one version of a five-sense meditation, a grounding technique that can get you back into the present moment. Minaa B., a therapist and author of *Owning Our Struggles*, suggests another grounding technique called an environmental scan, which entails mentally reminding yourself where you are. Think, *Right now I'm sitting in my bedroom* or *Right now I'm standing in the park.* "When we're in a state of presence, we can realize that [anxiety] that feels so threatening doesn't really exist," says Minaa B.

2. **Cold therapy.** Cold can help activate the parasympathetic nervous system, the nerve network that helps you relax. One 2018 study showed cold exposure can help slow your heart rate. You don't have to dunk yourself into icy waters to gain the benefits either. Try placing a cold pack on your forehead, splashing your face with cold water, or holding an ice cube.

3. **Deep breathing.** Deep breathing is another very simple and effective method of activating that para-sympathetic nervous system. Plus, your breath is a shortcut to the present moment—it's always with you. Try taking a deep, slow breath. If one deep breath doesn't cut it, Giscombé says you can always take another. Here are a few other ways to level up your breathing:

- **Box breathing.** Inhale for four counts. Hold for four counts. Exhale for four counts. You can combine this with a visualization of each inhale and each exhale tracing sides of a box.

- **Exhaling for longer than your inhale.** Breathe in for a count of four and then exhale for a count of eight.

- **Counting to ten.** Simply count your inhales and exhales. Inhale on the one, exhale on the

Breathe in.   Breathe out.

two. Inhale on three, exhale on four, and so on. Continue until you get to ten. Repeat as necessary.

- **Breathe in/breathe out.** If you're game for a visualization, try this variation of a lojong teaching. If you're in distress, imagine inhaling that pain on your in breath. It's uncomfortable, I know. But you're not holding on to it for long. On your out breath, imagine pushing out ease. Not necessarily positive vibes or even happiness—just ease. I think of it like washing the emotion. You might still feel the negative feeling but now it's scrubbed clean of judgment.

4. **Healthy distractions.** Turn off your brain with something absorbing. Listen to music you love, knit, color, cook. "That can be a form of distraction, but also be something that pours back into [you]," says Minaa B. A few glasses of wine might feel like a quick fix, but alcohol impacts serotonin levels, which can often worsen anxiety. Healthy distraction is how I started to learn embroidery. When I became absorbed with learning French knots and lazy daisy stitches, the anxiety that felt permanently burrowed in my chest would start to break up in my body. Ask yourself what your options are for a distracting activity *right now*. What are you willing to do? Britt Frank says that reframing what you *could* do to what you are *willing*

to do helps decision-making feel more manageable. Because you technically *could* do almost anything. "What am I willing to do?" gets you out of the paradox of choice with a smaller pool of choices.

5. **Move**. Go on a walk, take a dance break, get up and stretch. Movement helps activate dopamine, serotonin, and noradrenaline. Dr. Wendy Suzuki, a neuroscientist at New York University, has found in her research even short bursts of movement can lower anxiety levels.

Try one or perhaps a combination of these techniques. Maybe doing watercolors while deep breathing with an ice pack on your neck could be your jam. The point here isn't necessarily to feel better but to de-escalate the heat of the emotion. Deal with what's happening in the present moment and try not to go to the "why" of it all. *Why do I feel this way? Why am I so upset? What exact moment from my childhood led me to feel this way?* "You don't walk up to a burning building and ask, 'Why is it on fire?'" says Frank. "You put the fire out and you figure out the 'why' later." When your prefrontal cortex is back in working order, then you can engage in self-talk and introspection. Your mindfulness practice can help get your thinking brain back online.

Let's play out a scenario. Say you are invited to a dinner party. You put on your nice outfit, stop by the liquor store for a bottle of wine, and slap on your best party smile when greeted at the door. Then as dinner is served, it becomes very clear you're the only single person there. Everyone is paired up around the table with their significant other. You get wedged into a corner seat that doesn't have quite enough room. All the conversation seems to be about a couple things: trips that *we* are taking, plans for *our* wedding, or the holidays with *our* families. You're asked a few perfunctory questions about your work, but then the whole table wants to talk about your dating life. You feel like a specimen, not a guest. Later, while you're walking home, tears start to fall down your face. How could mindfulness help here? To be honest, I would likely let myself cry for a bit. No shame in walking and crying in public. I've practically made an art of it. But after the initial release of emotion, a curious mind can be brought in. You can use the technique of noting:

I notice that I'm feeling sad. I notice that I'm tearful.

A curious mind is a nonjudgmental mind. The practice of noting is going to help create a little distance between you and your big emotion. Once you have a bit of space, it is easier to self-soothe. Practicing creating distance is not forcing yourself into happiness if you're feeling sad. In fact, doing so might backfire. "I have seen this anecdotally, personally, and clinically. The number one contributor to being emotionally dysregulated is lying to ourselves," says Britt Frank. Feeling the feeling is the quickest path to emotional regulation, continues Frank.

So let's say you've used the noting technique and managed to get a little mental distance from the feeling—now you can engage your thoughts. What kinds of stories are you telling yourself at this moment? Are you ascribing good or bad qualities to your emotions? Instead, try to engage that nonjudgmental curious mind again. Giscombé recommends asking yourself questions like "What am I thinking right now in this moment? Is that thought really true?" Because often the narratives we tell ourselves about ourselves aren't exactly true; they have been constructed and embellished over time. We add commentary like "*I am unlovable*" or "*I am always going to be alone*" until it takes up most of the page. A little mindful fact-checking can help you gain wisdom and edit your story to better reflect reality.

Asking yourself what you're thinking right now in this moment might look like this: *What was it about tonight that caused this reaction? Is it because that party was all couples? Or was it because the couples were excluding me from the conversation at first? Or because everyone wanted to talk about my dating life when they know I'm on all the apps and I hate it? It was all these things—I am sad because the experience made me feel like an outsider.*

This neutral examination of your feelings combined with paying attention on purpose is powerful because once you've slowed down and have some data, you can seek out an alternative path.

Again, it's important here to not get caught up in self-judgment or *shoulds*. Don't feel like you *should* suck it up or *shouldn't* feel sad. Nothing makes me want to cry more than when I'm trying to force myself not to cry. Focus on what you actually need. Perhaps you need to text another single friend (or your mom) to talk it out. Or plan to meet up with friends you know won't talk about dating. Taking the time to feel your feelings and mindfully assess what you need doesn't change your emotions, but the intensity of them will likely lessen. Because now you've got some perspective and a plan.

Acceptance of emotions

Feeling bad, well, feels bad. I know that I sometimes run away from feeling uncomfortable by bingeing too much TV or scrolling mindlessly through social media. But having emotions, even negative ones, is part of the human experience. Here again, the tool of practicing acceptance can help. This can look as simple as thinking to yourself, *This is happening right now. I'm accepting that this bad feeling is happening.* A straightforward, nonjudgmental declaration. "It doesn't mean you have to love it," says Giscombé. "But if you want things to shift, you have to first accept it." This also doesn't mean accepting injustice or harm as inevitable or permanent; it means accepting your emotions as your *current* reality and moving forward with your rational mind.

Resisting negative emotions only prolongs suffering. Acceptance requires some patience, and a willingness to sit with discomfort. But it's a practice, Giscombé reminds me. You have endless opportunities to work toward it.

When it's all just not working

It's possible you try all these techniques and still feel like shit. You might take all the deep breaths in the world and still want to throw this book across the room. That's okay! You do not have to feel good. Bad days and bad moods will inevitably happen. "Your life isn't a performance," psychotherapist Meghan Watson told me. "You're not just on this earth to constantly be optimized for positivity. You're not here to constantly be in a state of joy." Everything is temporary. Bad days can turn into neutral days. Good days can turn into sad ones. All emotions ebb and flow.

What's helpful, always, is self-compassion. There are three main tenets of self-compassion, according to researcher Kristin Neff: self-kindness, common humanity, and mindfulness. If you feel bad about being single, an example of these three tenets could be thinking to yourself *It's okay to feel down sometimes* (self-kindness), *Other people feel bad sometimes, too—I'm not the only one* (common humanity), and *I notice I'm feeling sad. I feel it in my chest* (mindfulness).

All this takes practice. Think about it like a baby learning to walk—we expect that the baby is going to fall down a lot, and we don't judge them when they do. "I should hope that you're not like, 'Get up, baby!'" says Giscombé. "We're still giving them that love and that encouragement, but we're not adding that judgment to it." When you fall down in life, try to give yourself that same compassion.

Self-compassion isn't self-pity, self-indulgence, or self-esteem, according to Neff. You're not piling onto yourself nor are you forcing toxic positivity, which sometimes gets lumped in with self-compassion. It makes my skin crawl to hear "turn that frown upside down." Sometimes that frown should be there! Because life does throw hardships our way.

Watson told me that we can (and should) be realistic with self-compassion. There's no need to do anything that feels out of step with who you are. "Can you be compassionate without being positive 100 percent?" asks Watson. The answer is yes. You can go back to the emotions-as-data framework and you can be neutral. You can use this data to make choices that will help you self-soothe.

Getting specific about emotions

SECONDARY EMOTIONS

Let's return to singlehood. How can you best live between the two spaces of wanting a partner, if that's what you want, and knowing you don't need one? Well, first, get clear about what you're actually feeling, which often involves what are known as primary and secondary emotions.

Sometimes a longing for a relationship would arise out of nowhere and I might think *I hate that I feel this way, I hate that I don't have someone. God, this is so pathetic.* The primary emotion—the main presenting emotion—is obvious: sadness. The secondary emotion is a reaction to the primary emotion. My belief system—the stories I've constructed about what it means to feel sad about this situation—are the root of the secondary emotion. In this case, that would be shame. Secondary emotions often point to how our experiences color our feelings. I felt bad about not having someone because my culture and my beliefs were telling me I should feel bad about that. Changing the secondary emotion involves challenging beliefs.

In the process of untangling all the myths I've absorbed about singleness, I was working on changing that secondary emotion from shame to acceptance. *Sure, I'm home on a Friday night but that's okay. I've had a long week at work where I was in a million meetings and some quiet time is what I need right now.*

Teasing out the secondary emotion was helpful to me. Questioning my beliefs about feeling sad or lonely helped me better decode where my negative feelings were coming from and work on changing them.

ANXIETY

Simply put, anxiety is the anticipation of a future threat (real or imagined). And, wow, there are so many things to be anxious about. Anxiety around a task or a concrete event is uncomfortable but manageable for me. The days leading up to a certification exam, a public speaking event, or a medical appointment can be anxiety inducing, but there's a specific end date when a distinct sense of relief will follow.

But the anxiety around amorphous uncertainty—for me, that's the real killer. When people (often partnered folks) would tell me, "You're going to meet someone! I just know it!" I'd half smile and think, *You don't know that.* Sometimes that fact sat well with me. I'd shrug off the well-meaning comment and move on with my day. Cut to me trying to relax at home with a book at some later time. Suddenly, a tightness would start in my chest, small and then radiating out. I'd be unable to focus on my book, I'd feel worried. I knew I was anxious but about what, exactly?

Then a flash of the earlier conversation would hit, "You're going to meet someone!" Next thing I knew, the tightness in my chest had convinced me that I had to decide—soon!— whether I'd want kids as a single parent and, you know, maybe I was going to die alone. These are some big leaps!

The feeling of anxiety is terrible. But the physiology of anxiety is actually designed to protect us. Britt Frank thinks of it as a superpower. "Everyone hates that," she told me. Anxious feelings might feel like a threat (they aren't called panic attacks for nothing), but anxiety is a signal—another one of those helpful data points.

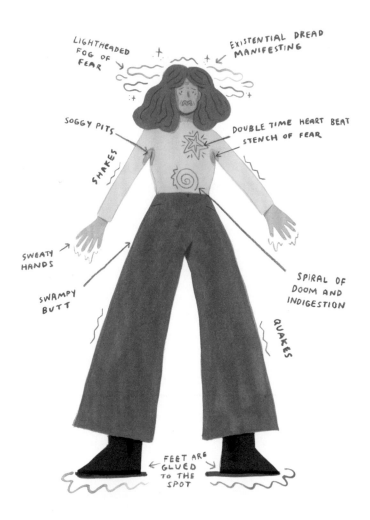

"When a smoke alarm goes off, you don't say that 'the smoke alarm is attacking the house!' The noise is really, really aggravating, and if you didn't know what was going on, you would think something dangerous is happening," Frank told me. "But anxiety is the smoke alarm of the brain." As someone who's both struggled with anxiety and used to have a finicky smoke alarm that would go off every time I so much as preheated my oven, I feel this.

How can we deal with anxiety? Like all negative feelings, you can try some of the de-escalation techniques from earlier in this chapter. Frank thinks of it as climbing down the anxiety ladder to emotional regulation:

THE ANXIETY LADDER

- Anxiety at the top of the ladder. (Free-floating worry with no origin. An abstract feeling.)
- Fear. (Heart rate is elevated, sweaty palms, dry mouth. Anxiety with a point of origin.)
- Worry. (Same body sensations as anxiety and fear but at a lesser intensity and with a clear point of origin.)
- Stress. (Uncomfortable feeling with or without a point of origin. Not as heated as fear.)
- Regulation. (Acceptance of emotion and worry. Able to make choices and take healthy action.)

Here's what that looks like in practice. You want to down-grade your anxiety to something more manageable. First, validate the anxiety. *This feeling sucks* (there is that acceptance part again!). Now shrink it down into something more specific. For me, the fear of not being partnered isn't *really* about dying alone. (To be frank, life has a 100 percent mortality rate and any of us can die at any time, so let's just rid ourselves of that concern, shall we?) My anxiety was more about the fear of not being supported. Here's a point of origin, bringing me one step down the rickety anxiety ladder. Sure, it's stressful to not be supported, but would that actually be my reality? Would all my friends and loved ones disappear entirely from me later in life? Likely no. Another step down the ladder, and my feet would be on the ground. Now I can make rational choices. I could thank my brain's smoke detector, hit the silence button, and move on.

ANGER ICEBERGS

While we're under the hood of our emotional minds, let's take a quick look at anger. Anger can seemingly come out of nowhere. I could feel completely fine doing all the grocery shopping for my single person life but then have a day when my boss calls to talk about a stressful work question, my grocery bag breaks on the way home and the tomato sauce crashes to the sidewalk, and so does my patience about being single. Boss gets a snippy response and I'm in a bad mood for the rest of the day.

It's helpful here to imagine an anger iceberg. It's a concept from the Gottman Institute, a research leader in healthy

communication and relationships. Poking out of the water is the emotion of anger. It's the most visible. But underneath the surface are all the other emotions that contribute to the anger like anxiety, rejection, disappointment, and so on. Let's go back to the spilled sidewalk marinara. Do I feel like I don't have enough support in my day-to-day tasks? Am I sad that I don't have an extra set of hands to carry all these groceries? To deal with these kinds of frustrating emotions, validate yourself—let yourself feel angry. Next, think about how you can tend to your needs. (Are you sensing a theme?) Perhaps ask a friend to buddy up when running errands. Borrow a can of crushed tomatoes from your neighbor to make a replacement sauce. Call your boss back and say you need some more support on the work problem. If you're hitting an anger iceberg, remember to ask yourself, "what is this really about?"

DEALING WITH ENVY

Slipping into the comparison game when you're single is easy. Sometimes all it takes is a couple sharing an inside joke or a knowing glance to trigger the green-eyed monster. But comparison (say it with me) is the thief of joy. (Don't tell my editor, but clichés have become alarmingly more relatable as I've gotten older.)

Since our goal is to get specific about our feelings, let's define envy and jealousy. They are twin flames that often get confused. Envy is wanting something you don't have—feeling riled up when you see yet another couple holding hands while you're just trying to run errands. Jealousy is being anxious that something you have is going to be taken from you—how you might feel when a friend starts spending more time with their new boyfriend and has less time for you.

Envy and jealousy come with a lot of negative baggage, but they are just emotions. "It's okay to acknowledge that I want what other people have," says therapist Minaa B. "It is okay to see other people living the life that you hoped you could live, and it's okay to desire that."

Though envy *can* lead to some problematic behavior, potentially disrupting relationships and friendships. You might not be hiding that annoyed look or irritated tone as well as you think. Be mindful of how you treat people when you're feeling envious. It's not okay to disrespect a friend because their life is unfolding differently than yours.

One way to check envy? Ask yourself "How can I work toward the things that I desire?" suggests Minaa B.

I know I promised no dating advice in this book. But if you want to date, date! For me, one way of dealing with partnership envy meant staying open to dating. But in a more relaxed way than I had been. In order to not fall into the trap of filling up every free weeknight with a drink with a stranger, I drastically reduced the number of first dates on my calendar. I put restrictions on my dating app use, which is just good for anyone's mental health. I worked to give myself all the fun things that I assumed I had to be in partnership to have. Trips abroad? Yes. Nice dinners? Done. A beautiful home? Check this decor, darling.

Another trick is to reroute the envy. Let's say your single friend gets paired up. There's a particular ache when that happens—it's great to see them happy but, damn it, that was your single buddy who you did single things with! You can go internal and think about what it means for you. Or you can choose to depersonalize the moment and focus on wanting to be happy for your friend in that moment. Start by trying some self-talk. Hung suggests something like "I just really want to be happy for my friend now." If the envy is still tempting you, Hung also recommends appealing to your values: "What kind of friend do I want to be? How do I want to show up for this person?"

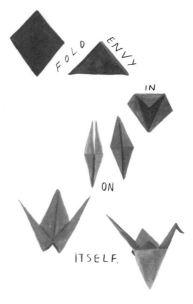

Folding the envy in on itself can make room to see the bigger picture.

NEAR ENEMY

The near enemy is a Buddhist concept to describe the sneaky cousin of an emotion that tricks you into thinking you're experiencing something positive while really sabotaging you into an unhelpful place. One time I was dating someone and I was anxious about how infrequently they were texting (okay, I'll admit it, this has happened way more than once). This particular guy would wait just long enough to answer a simple question to make my anxiety go wild. (Really, how many hours does it take to confirm you're on for dinner? I don't care how busy your job is—we're all busy!) I thought I was experiencing love, or at least its initial stirrings. I really like him, so I need him to answer me! But I wasn't feeling love. I was experiencing the near enemy of love—attachment. I was too caught up in thinking I had such a great connection with this person that I didn't see how that "love" was fear-based. Which is not to say this guy shouldn't have been texting me back, or I shouldn't have just moved on faster,

but this near enemy of love had me mistaken about what it was I was feeling. Here are some more examples adapted from the work of writer and Buddhist teacher Jack Kornfield.

- *Equanimity's near enemy is indifference.*
- *Loving-kindness's near enemy is attachment.*
- *Compassion's near enemy is pity.*
- *Shared joy or appreciation's near enemies are jealousy or comparison.*

When you aren't partnered, it's not uncommon for the near enemy of equanimity to show up: indifference. Indifference isn't calm acceptance, it's thinking "It never works out so why bother dating" or "I hate feeling lonely, but I guess I have to get used to it since I'll be lonely forever." Throwing your hands up in surrender doesn't actually give you peace, it only makes it harder to weather emotional storms when they inevitably come. When you spot this near enemy in your presence, remember to slow down and question the story you're telling yourself. Is it actually true? Instead of pretending you don't have feelings, can you be vulnerable and listen to your emotions?

You can also use your knowledge of the near enemy to get better support from loved ones. Think about when someone who's coupled up hears about your latest string of bad dates and says something like, "I can't imagine being out in the dating pool again! I don't know what I would do!" That's not compassion, it's its near enemy, pity. Being able to detect a near enemy coming from others can help us adjust our own response. Perhaps you could respond, "I think you would be frustrated like I am. Right now I just need your support, not a comparison."

There's a pattern in the advice in this chapter. When you have an emotion, slow it down and figure out what you need. Think about what your emotion is telling you—what might be its near enemy? And how can you turn toward the nourishing version of that emotion instead? "The more that we can be intentional about our choice and feel good about it, the more confidence we will feel about our decisions," Hung told me. "By seeing what [the emotions are] there for, you're kind of learning to live with it and not trying to make it go away. Because if emotions went away, that means we're not human anymore."

Managing emotions isn't about crushing them—or even controlling them. During my conversation with Kessonga Giscombé, he picked up a snow globe off his desk. "So, with

strong emotions, it's kind of like a snow globe, right?" He shook the snow globe. Glittery white flecks obscured the stacked rocks at the center. "It's just a whirlwind, and it's just going and going," Giscombé said. "But once you pause and you stop for a moment and allow that strong emotion to just settle, [the snow] doesn't disappear, right?"

It didn't. But I noticed I felt calmer watching the snow globe's snowstorm subside. The miniature stack of rocks inside came a bit more into focus. The rageful blur now felt peaceful.

"With that settling, that's when the clarity comes."

MAKE HELPFUL LISTS

- Write down five activities that help keep you grounded in the present moment, maybe journaling or doing a craft or just looking around you.
- Write down three things that usually comfort you when you're feeling emotionally heated.
- Make a go-to plan for those days you just need to feel bad.

JOURNAL PROMPTS

- Think of times when your emotions gave you helpful data. What kinds of choices did you make?

- Write about an emotion you have a hard time accepting. What makes it difficult to regulate? What triggers it?

- When you feel a big emotion, what would acceptance of that emotion look like for you?

- What stories do you think you're telling yourself about negative emotions like anger or anxiety?

PRACTICE

- Try mindfulness in tiny doses.

- Commit to doing a task mindfully for just two minutes. Try really bringing your awareness to all the sensations you experience when you shower, brush your teeth, eat something, walk down the street, cook. If your mind drifts, notice that drifting without judgment and tune in again.

- Try to note everything around you in your environment. Mentally list what you see: the desk, the pen, the chair, the rug. With practice you can more readily reach for this technique when in a state of heated emotion.

- When you're in the middle of a joyous event, pay attention to it. Note the friends who might be present, think about how your body feels, tune into the general vibe. Savor it.

- Make sure you are mindful of your basic needs. Are you getting enough sleep? Are you eating enough? Had enough water today? What other factors might affect your emotional state?

6

Intentional Friendships and Building Community

MY MOTHER HAD TO GET SURGERY WHILE I WAS writing this book. She had spondylosis, which caused one of the disks in her spine to jut forward. The condition left her with horrible sciatica pain and her doctor told her she'd be a good candidate for surgery to correct it. I offered to come stay with her during her recovery, which her doctor said would be short.

"Are you sure you only need me for those few days?" I asked her on the phone.

"Really, I should be fine!" she assured me. "Your aunt will be here. You just need to take me to the hospital that

Wednesday and then you can leave that weekend." She had heard from multiple people who had similar surgeries that the recovery was a breeze. My mom was already fantasizing about the brisk walks she'd be taking in no time.

Although the surgery was routine and not invasive as back surgeries go, we were in for a shock. In the hospital, she was calm and feeling good. But as soon as she tried to get out of the car when I brought her home, I knew this recovery would not be as easy as we thought. Even with a cane she struggled to walk a few feet. We quickly had to switch to the walker. She cried in pain when she sat down. The look of strain on her face scared me.

They give you the good painkillers through an IV in the hospital, but we were home now. Also, it turns out there are a lot of different kinds of back surgeries so our anecdotal research wasn't exactly applicable to her situation. My mom spent those first twenty-four hours at home moaning in pain. She was unable to bend or twist, meaning my aunt and I had to help her move in and out of bed, dress, and assist her with other necessary functions that made her blush. My aunt had a seven-page list of medications and she slept in the same bed as my mother so she could administer them in the middle of the night and help with any nighttime bathroom runs.

Those few days of post-surgery help turned into a few weeks. I did grocery runs, cooked meals, and emptied the dishwasher so my aunt didn't have to worry about doing housework after caring for my mom. My dog Margo also pitched in as much as she could by giving my mom kisses every morning. Thankfully, my mom didn't have any additional complications. But the level of support needed was much higher than we expected.

My mom had been widowed for eighteen years by this time and my aunt has never married. We've all lived independently for years. Suddenly, three typically self-sufficient women were in need not only of one another, but our communities as well.

Our family friend Margie, a former nurse, came over and edited our caretaking routine. (Note: You want to get ahead of the pain with properly prescribed meds, not wait until it's bad.) My mom's friends Carol and Gerry arrived with a big basket of pork, salad, and fresh peaches and tomatoes from the nearby orchard. The house phone rang all day with friends checking in on her while others dropped by when my mother's pain levels allowed her to receive visitors. Charlene, a friend my mom has known since they were in ninth grade together in Fairmont, West Virginia, came to stay for a few nights while my aunt had to attend an out-of-state funeral.

Whenever I comment on how my mom does nice things for her friends or for me, she usually responds, "It's just what you do." Sure. But this kind of community care didn't appear from nowhere. I know it's because my mom and aunt have spent a lifetime building and nurturing a network of mutual support. It takes intention and effort to not only build close friendships but maintain them. And it takes a high level of care and compassion to keep the kind of friends who will help you change a bandage from a surgery incision.

A lot of times being single feels like you're on the outside of something. It can feel like a Dickensian scene with part-

nered people cozy and warm by their hearth of coupledom and singles looking in from out in the cold. But singles aren't exiled. Instead, single people are standing on fertile ground, able to plant the seeds for exactly how they want their lives to unfold. We get to choose the kind of community and support we want in the garden of our lives.

We've spent this whole book learning to love our own company. Now it's time to look outward. As we've discussed, singlehood doesn't mean being alone. And just because you can do so much on your own doesn't mean you have to. You can get creative and diversify your connections.

In this chapter, we learn how to prioritize friendship. If seeing my mother recover from surgery has taught me anything, it's that we need more than one system of support in our lives.

Friendship isn't a "bonus"—
it's essential

Because marriage and romantic love can be seen as the strongest, most worthy type of relationship, friends, we've been told, seem not as essential. But friendship needn't be some kind of consolation prize for not having romantic partnership. A friendship-centered life is not a second-rate life. In fact, a life built around friendship can be one of the healthiest and most satisfying there is.

In one of the longest studies conducted on adult life, the Harvard Study of Adult Development tracked the lives of over seven hundred men over the course of nearly eighty years. The study asked participants about all different facets of their lives: work, home life, health, etc. A key conclusion, the fourth director of the study, Harvard psychiatrist Robert Waldinger, and his team found, was that good relationships keep us happier and healthier. And not just good romantic relationships—positive friendships, family relationships, casual acquaintances: All of them were beneficial.

People who had community ties, they found, lived longer. Good social connections can help reduce loneliness and stress, which we know can lead to poor health outcomes. Another study, this one a six-year research study of over seven hundred Swedish men, found that being socially integrated had a protective effect from coronary heart-disease events. Having a life partner, they found, did not have as strong of a protective effect. Friendships are also important as we age. In a survey of 280,000 people, professor of psychology William Chopik at Michigan State University found that friendships in older age had a bigger impact on happiness than family.

We've been sold this fantasy that only married couples have access to the benefits of close connection. That single people need to "hurry up" and find a partner before it's "too late." Women in particular are pressured to think about what age is the upper limit before they "give up" (think Meg Ryan in *When Harry Met Sally* sobbing about how an ex of hers is getting married and she's about to be single at forty even though she's still thirty-two). Part of the cultural fear around singleness is the threat of spinsterhood for women and isolation. But those fears are simply not based in reality.

Singles are an often-ignored source of strong community and friendship. The cultural stigma about singles obscures the truth: Not only do singles have fulfilling friendships, but they also often have more of them. Singles tend to have more social connections than married people, according to researchers Natalia Sarkisian and Naomi Gerstel. Another study from researcher Elyakim Kislev found the same and, further, that singles can also surpass married couples in happiness if they are particularly proactive about their friendships. I believe that's true because singles are typically naturals at cultivating lots of different kinds of connections. The skill of finding community in multiple places is a gift.

Friendships give you a sense of belonging, joy, relief, and comfort. Part of single life is relishing these connections. Let's work to supercharge our friendships.

Extending your network

Close friendship is special and precious. But we can't be super close with every person we meet. There are going to be a variety of relationships in your life—and singlehood provides a great opportunity to get the most out of all of them.

Think about the person you always get bagels from on the weekend, or the bartender who's starting to recognize you at your local pub. Or a fellow dog owner in your neighborhood who knows your dog's name but not yours (who can blame them?). These are what are known as "weak ties," a term coined in a 1973 paper by sociologist Mark Granovetter. That quippy joke you share with your barista might not feel particularly meaningful, but that low-stakes kind of connection can improve our happiness and sense of belonging according to research by Gillian Sandstrom, senior lecturer of psychology at the University of Sussex.

This isn't permission to monopolize the time of the farm stand guy who's just trying to move apples during the Sunday

morning rush. Rather, just be open to interacting briefly with those weak ties in your community. Being friendly costs you nothing, as my mom says, and you might both walk away with a little emotional boost.

If the weak tie is someone in your direct community, those interactions might expand your world a bit. Maybe casual chitchat with the local librarian leads to you learning about a cool event where you meet like-minded folks. All those "hey, how are yous" with your neighbor might lead to backyard cocktails. At the very least, you might glean some good neighborhood gossip. (The owner of Pluto the pit bull told me all the drama about the construction on our street. Permits about balconies are more entertaining than you might think.)

If you want to up your dose of these casual interactions, get involved within your community. Volunteer for mutual aid efforts, show up for cleanup events, bring used books to the library drive. Research from Bonnie Le, an assistant professor of psychology at University of Rochester, found that being communally oriented leads to "greater self-esteem, greater satisfaction and love in their relationships, and greater love for humanity in daily life."

Pre-COVID, I'd say I knew a few of my neighbors. My next-door neighbors were great about waving me over for a glass of wine when I was sitting alone reading on the roof. But I certainly didn't know anyone who lived in the next building over, let alone on the next block. And then I brought home a puppy. Suddenly, I knew everyone. Baby Margo prancing around the neighborhood looking like an adorable stuffed animal got people's attention. I wasn't just sharing a passing hello with my neighbors, I was having repeated contact. Now I could get the updates about my building's malfunctioning elevator from my neighbor as I passed him on a walk with his dog, Mac, or enjoy a quick laugh with Mabel's people as our dogs engaged in a playful sidewalk tussle.

One day in front of my place, a dog with Farrah Fawcett hair trotted up to Margo. His owner gave me a big smile and we chatted as our pups played. Turns out, our dogs were pretty close in age and they were both on the small side, so they were well suited for playmates.

"I just moved back to the area. I live two blocks away. Here's my number if you ever want to stop by for pup playtime in the backyard," the owner told me.

I was desperate to socialize puppy Margo. And since this was October 2020, I was also hungry for human socialization. And this neighbor had a COVID-safe venue? Incredible.

Backyard puppy playdates turned into backyard wine nights. Which turned into coffee runs, which naturally led to martini and oyster night. Last spring, she invited me to her family's cabin in Shenandoah, where we took in the view, just the two of us (and our dogs).

Her forwardness that day on the street inspired me. When I noticed a fluffy Maltipoo taking a shining to Margo, I asked the owner for *her* number. We didn't become weekend-away type friends, but we often lean on each other for dog care in a pinch. These two connections started similarly and ended up at different levels of closeness, but they are both meaningful.

Forge friendships with intention

There have been times in history when platonic love was seen as more pure than spousal love. The meaning of platonic love often gets muddled, argues professor and author Marisa G. Franco. Fifteenth-century Italian scholar Marsilio Ficino, who first elaborated the concept of platonic love, conceived of it as worthy on its own and not as "romantic love undergoing subtraction," Franco writes in her book *Platonic: How the Science of Attachment Can Help You Make—and Keep—Friends.* Platonic love to Ficino is being in the divine light of another soul that brings you awe.

"Friends are looking for ways to love you. You have to give them the opportunity."

— Marisa Franco

The takeaway here is that to attain all these wonderful benefits of friendship, we need to not only decide that friendship matters to us but also intentionally cultivate and deepen our connections. Take a second to think: How are you spending your social time? Does it feel like a to-do list of obligations or meaningful time with people who delight you? Do you have friends you can count on? Do you have friends who support you wholeheartedly? De-emphasizing the rat race of dating and putting your energy into your friendships will clarify who you want to spend your time with.

Sometimes that means a realigning of our social ties. That doesn't mean only seeking out singles if you're single. Married people shouldn't only have married friends, either—a diversity of connections is crucial no matter your relationship status.

You might find that some people aren't as psyched as you are to make this commitment to friendship. Flaking will happen. Schedules won't align. But don't be discouraged. There are others who are just as ready to invest deeply in friendship as you. There's a concept in social psychology called the matching hypothesis Franco told me about. It's the idea that people are more likely to come together if both parties find each other equally socially desirable and attractive. If in this period of investing in friendship, you find some people turn away—let them. You will find those who are on the same page turning toward you.

How do we actually make committed and nourishing friendships happen? It takes a certain amount of social fitness, a term coined by Robert Waldinger and his colleagues, to maintain friendships. Think about it—we can't just exercise once a year and expect our physical and mental health to be taken care of. Friendships require maintenance, true, but also intentionality and creativity. Here are some ideas to build those social muscles:

BE THE STARTER

One summer I was lounging at the community pool (DC's public pool network is stellar) when I peeked over the edge of my book. I saw a coworker of mine in the water. We had the kind of connection where we weren't close, but we had a lot of mutual friends, so we always chatted each other up at a party. While tempted to bury myself in my book and let myself go unnoticed in the crowd, I instead waded into the literal waters to say hello. After the initial "how is your summer going" exchange, I asked about her boyfriend. "Oh, we broke up a long time ago."

Embarrassment colored my cheeks. But she seemed unfazed and still up for chatting. I saw an opening. *A fellow single woman in DC. She might be a good friend to invest in.* We spent the rest of that summer texting each other invites to dog-walking dates, rooftop drinks, and lots more pool time. She taught me how to bedazzle clothing and was my plus-one to my first post-COVID lockdown concert. She could have stayed just a coworker, but now she was my friend I could hug and cry together with over the beauty of getting to experience live music at the 9:30 Club again.

One of the simplest ways to feel socially connected is to be the initiator. Leading the charge with social invitations helps in a few ways. For one, it increases your chances of deepening the friendships you want to pursue. It also gives you agency so you're not subject to experiencing FOMO. And, perhaps a bit selfishly, it means you often get to do the activity you actually want to do. This is why I love hosting friends for dinner—I have fun being the architect of the evening but I also get to serve the exact food I want and I don't have to leave my apartment. It's a win-win for me.

Another way being the initiator helps build connection is that being included makes people feel good. There's something so truly heartwarming about getting a text from a newer friend asking you to hang after that initial meeting. In his book *The Art of Community*, author Charles H. Vogl writes that invites have the power to resolve the pervasiveness of loneliness that has caused a "crisis of belonging" today. Even a casual invite for a quick coffee helps to establish both you and your friend within a shared community.

If you're newly single, you're in a good position to take the initiative. Marisa Franco told me that it's a good idea to look for "transitioners"—people who are newly single, divorced, or just going through a big life change like a move. Transitioners are more receptive to invitations and are often easier to find through meetups and such. Or you can start to think about who in your life values similar activities and build out time to gather from there. Set up a monthly board game night with your fellow Wingspan enthusiasts. Get the friends who always talk romance novels with you to do a book club. Host a standing Sunday dinner.

For those kinds of more structured events, make sure to have a clear purpose. Priya Parker, in her book *The Art of Gathering*, pushes people to think more deeply about why they organize. After all, a meeting that happens every week because "that's what we've always done" doesn't really have a compelling reason to last. Parker writes that reasons to gather are often bland and uninspired. Instead, she suggests you "take the reasons you think you are gathering . . . and keep drilling below them. Ask why you're doing it. Every time you get to another, deeper reason, ask why again. Keep asking why until you hit a belief or value." This exercise helps clarify who you want to include. You might decide to host a semiregular group of single women for a meetup. On the surface, the purpose might be to get together with people in a similar situation. But by Parker's standards, that's just more of a casual gathering. An intentional reason for this group to get together is your shared values that single people deserve to not always feel like the third wheel. This meetup would be a night where you don't have to talk about dating (or at least don't have to pretend you're not annoyed with it). That's a better reason to gather.

If you don't have the means or the will to host at your place, do not fear. "Hospitality is a mindset," writes psychologist Lisa Kentgen and author of *The Practice of Belonging*. Giving the gift of your attention is more essential than opening your home. A simple way to do this is by being interested in people. Robert Waldinger, the Harvard psychiatrist behind the Adult Development Study mentioned earlier, suggests you approach even well-established connections afresh. He notes that "curiosity is a way to acknowledge people," so even if you've known a friend since childhood, try asking them something you've never asked them before.

Friendships are often built in a string of small, spontaneous moments. That means every outing for a friendship doesn't have to be an elaborately planned themed day (though as someone who had hosted a twelve-hour rom-com film festival, those do have their merits). To Kentgen, a life devoted to the mindset of hospitality means creating "space in our schedules and lives for spontaneous invitations and lingering conversations."

All of this is to say, depending on what kind of time and energy you have to give, there is a level of initiation you can offer. Make the gesture and watch the magic.

WHEN IN DOUBT, SUPPORT

The mark of a good friendship is the dance of generosity. I come to your neighborhood across town when I've got a more flexible schedule and you bring dinner over one night when I'm too stressed to cook. There are seasons in life when someone might need more support, but when the friendship is good, no one is keeping score.

This is why we need to show up for our friends. They need us and we need them. Showing up is not to be confused with giving excessively. Franco writes in her book that giving too readily in a martyr-like way comes from a more selfish motivation: to be liked. And any people pleaser knows that giving too much of your time, energy, and resources breeds resentment. Instead, it is better to give in a way that feels meaningful to you and to your friend.

One way to embody this is to practice "shine theory." It's a term coined by the friends and collaborators Aminatou Sow and Ann Friedman. Shine theory is the practice of a "mutual, meaningful, over the long term" investment in a friend. In their book *Big Friendship: How We Keep Each Other Close,*  they write that shine theory is about asking yourself if someone can be a collaborator rather than a competitor. Instead of being envious when a friend gets a promotion while you've been having a tough job search, celebrate their win. When you finally land the gig you've been waiting for, that friend will be there to shine right back at you. When you have the space to help a friend with a contact, a piece of advice, or some insider knowledge, share what you can and help them succeed along with you.

I like to apply shine theory to my dating life. If you're actively dating, it can feel akin to a competitive job marketplace. Plus, the dating pool can be so small. I can't tell you how many friends of mine have been on dates with people I'd also met on dating apps. (*He's a lawyer? Who just moved here from California? Yeah, I think I know him . . .*) Instead of seeing single friends as competition, I chose to see them as collaborators. Their connection with a person does not mean my chances of meeting someone go down. It's better to support my friend and share in her delight than resent her. I also find it helpful to depersonalize these moments. I attended a wedding not long after getting dumped. I felt self-conscious that I was the single girl at a wedding. During the toasts talking about the couple and their love for one another, it hit me: *Today is not about me.* I went on to enjoy the rest of the night.

SHOW UP AND HELP OUT

A way to tap into this is to make loving overtures for friends. By that, I don't mean sexual advances, but romantic in that it relates to love. Think favors, errands, or activities often associated with a supportive romantic partner but not totally reserved for them.

Franco told me about a friend of hers who was returning from a trip to Mexico and needed a ride home. Her flight was landing past midnight. Franco winced at the prospect of a late-night airport pickup. She's much more of a morning person. "But I have to ask myself would I do this for a romantic partner? And I said yes." Funny how the idea of romantic love monopolizes acts devoid of all sexuality.

Make the effort—but know you are also allowed to ask for help, too. We tend to underestimate how much people will support us. Research finds that we often assume people will see our requests as an inconvenience. But the opposite is true: People feel good when they can help. The reality is that friends like helping friends. "What I have to do sometimes to get myself to ask for things from friends. Flip it: What if this friend asked me for this? How would I feel?" Franco told me. Well, I'd feel great! I love this because it asks us to call the bluff of our anxieties and awkward feelings. A simple reframing helps drop unhelpful defenses and leads to connection.

After a few rides to the emergency room, cat-sitting stints, and car trouble rescues, we all know the friends who can be best called upon and for what kind of support. Franco calls these diagnostic moments. These are data points to help us see how a friendship fares during moments of highest distress (a death, an injury, a heartbreak, a job loss) and highest joy (career milestones, a new pet, the completion of a creative project). Which friends make you feel the most seen and supported in both the highs and lows?

I have a personal rule. When I see someone who has also lost a parent—even if they are an acquaintance—I write them an email or send a card. I know how personal grief is, but even the smallest acknowledgment to a friend that you're thinking of them in a tough time is so powerful.

Showing up in hard times is important, but there's also evidence that celebrating with loved ones is good for our health as well. I happen to love my birthday. I often celebrate with a big, splashy gathering, but I know that makes many people shudder. Ask your friends their preferences for celebrations and make your own wishes known, too. Don't limit it to birthdays—celebrate the arrival of a friend's new guinea pigs, their completing the Pacific Crest Trail, the anniversary of your friendship, or a making it through the first month of a new job.

"I think some people struggle with friendship because they don't know how to let people love them," Franco told me. "They don't ask when they need something from a friend. For a lot of people, their friends are looking for ways to love you. You have to give them the opportunity."

Making rituals

A few years ago, I called upon my two friends Becky and Colleen for some help. I wanted to mark a new year with sparkles and bubbles, sure, but I was also seeking some guidance. It was December 2018 and I felt particularly single. I had thought I would have met someone by this point after my last relationship ended in early April (meanwhile, this ex had moved on after a mere two weeks and made this very known via Instagram). I was feeling stuck.

I asked if we could have a tarot night, one focused on forecasting the next year. Becky and Colleen came over with bags full of different kinds of decks. We took turns doing readings where we laid cards in a big circle, each card symbolizing a month of the year. Seeing their cards reminded me of how we all go through some of the same challenges, just shuffled in a different order. My reading had a lot of wands (Colleen likes to think of those as "vibes") and, as the overarching theme of the year, a nine of cups—a card of celebration. I didn't know what exactly I would be celebrating but I liked the spirit of it.

A few days later I was over at my mom's house. I was telling her about my little coven night and how meaningful it was to me; how I was excited to do it again the following year.

"Your dad used to do tarot, you know," she told me.

No, I didn't know. This didn't totally surprise me, though—my father once explained the pagan origins of Christmas during grace one holiday dinner. My dad passed away a week after I turned sixteen, so there was lots of information about him that disappeared after his death.

My mom went upstairs and came back with a classic Rider-Waite tarot deck. It was my father's. I was at a loss for words. I had been calling upon a ritual without even realizing it.

Ritual helps keep us grounded in what matters to us. It's also about finding pleasure among a community, writes Lisa Kentgen in *The Practice of Belonging*. "Collectively savoring the good things in life helps us move through its challenges with grace and resilience," she writes. If you're craving deeper community, start to develop deeper rituals.

Think back to chapter four, where we discussed our values. What kind of values do you want to bring to your community? Is it beauty? Justice? Spirituality? Service? From there, start to think about what would be a meaningful ritual that embodies those values. Is it an annual hike when the leaves start to change? Is it hosting an Oscar party every year with food inspired by the movies? Is it baking an intricate cake every year for the block party? Is it leading a group meditation for the new moon cycle? The length and formality of the ritual is flexible. The important thing is to lead with your values and share the experience. If your ritual makes you and your loved ones feel a sense of belonging, you will all be invested in continuing that ritual

BEAUTY.

SPIRITUALITY.

SERVICE.

JUSTICE.

and will be motivated to gather as a community more often.

Our culture likes to favor the rituals of couples. Bridal showers, weddings, anniversaries, baby showers—they are all lovely, but not everyone will get to be the center of them (or want to be). By creating time and space for celebrating a friend's promotion, taking a yearly trip, or gathering for a Friendsgiving, you push back against a culture that tells a single person "you don't deserve this communal love." Creating your own rituals as a single person helps you feel the affection of community and friends. Researcher Emily Langan at Wheaton College finds that close friendships need three main ingredients: ritual, assurances, and openness. Commemorating experiences with friends is crucial, she says.

You can also cultivate assurance and openness into your ritual by "strengthening" the ritual, as Charles H. Vogl puts it in *The Art of Community*. Strengthening means calling attention to the specialness of the moment. He gives the example of having different members of a family light a candle on a birthday cake and listing one thing they appreciate about the person that year. I always like to ask people on their birthdays what intention they want to set for the year ahead. It's a ritual that gives my friend a moment to reflect and it gives me insight about how they are feeling right now in their lives. Amping up a ritual doesn't mean spending a lot of money (I'm looking at you, out-of-control bachelorettes with a million party favors). It just means acknowledging that we are here together and isn't that special? Take a lesson from my New Year's tarot reading and tap into your celebratory nine of cups energy. Toast what and who you have around you.

Shifts in friendships

The reality is that people's lives are always changing and so are their priorities. A newly married friend might see friendships as an occasional bonus rather than a vital part of their life. A soon-to-be dad might be working overtime to help support his partner after finding out they are having twins. It's not just partnered people, either. You might find some of your single friends might not be in the headspace to invest as deeply as you. A friend who was great for frequent hangouts in your early twenties might now be focusing on starting her new business or another friend needs to prioritize building connections in their new city.

While it would be nice to cast a friendship in amber at its most intimate, that's not possible. Sometimes a friend's life morphs into something else before you're ready for it to change. The transition can feel like a loss.

But Marisa Franco told me that often people make assumptions about how busy a friend is going to be in a life transition. Let's take the classic example of a friend with a new baby. The single, child-free friend tends to think their new parent friend isn't going to have any time or want them to be around. But Franco says she often hears something similar from the person with the new baby.

Of course, there is the reality that kids just take time. But that doesn't mean you have to go no contact with the friend. "I've realized that it's important to include people, even if you think they're going to say no," Franco told me. She explains how she was setting up a group trip and extended the invite to her friends with kids, just to show she was thinking of them and that the door of friendship was still open.

Will the friendship look different over time? Likely. But just because a friendship changes doesn't mean it's spoiled forever. Franco urges people to look for mutuality in a friendship, especially when riding the wave of change. That means thinking about both your needs and your friend's needs. Then, figure out whose needs are more urgent right now and see if you are willing to be flexible. If you're willing to meet your friend at her home after she puts the kid to bed and it doesn't cause you to feel resentment later, then congrats—you are maintaining a friendship!

This doesn't mean the friend with the more urgent needs gets all the attention. You are also allowed to let your friend know when your needs in the friendship are important. You can tell your friend that this party celebrating your promotion is really important to you and you hope they can come or that you'd love to have a standing phone call. Or that you'd like to keep up with texting *Real Housewives* memes. If there's a commitment to reciprocity from both parties (just maybe in a new way), that's a friendship transition success.

I appreciate this approach of working together instead of making a relationship a zero-sum game. It's easy to get caught up in main character energy when the contours of a friendship are changing. *My friend is spending too much time at work with her new job—I feel like I never get to see her. Doesn't she know I need more social time now that I'm single?* Easy there. Understanding your needs is crucial, but we don't operate in a vacuum.

"We focus so much on self-healing that sometimes we don't realize when our ego is in the driver's seat and when we are acting in ways where we are making everything about us and forgetting about the needs of other people," Minaa B., therapist and author of *Owning Our Struggles*, told me. Maybe your friend is also craving more time with you but just needs a few more weeks to dig out of a work hole. Can you put time on the calendar and promise to stick to it? Working to be in communion with a friend you care about is better than giving up on the friendship.

"If we want to embody what healing looks like, we need to think about ourselves. But we also need to think about the people around us and the communities that we want to be a part of," Minaa B. told me. "Connection and togetherness are really what drives us forward."

Instead of operating from a place of "I can't offer this," try thinking about what you can give your friend. It's reciprocity theory: Setting an example of generosity will help them do the same. In a friendship transition, there is room for negotiation, says Franco. "I just tend to think there's often ways to fulfill both people's needs," she told me. "But we just don't talk about it enough to get to that place."

I know that sometimes a friendship will change in undesirable ways, even if you take all these steps. A friend might flat-out tell you that they are focusing on their family and partnership and no longer want to put energy into your friendship (it happens . . .). In those times, feel the grief but then look to your other connections. I guarantee that if you're someone putting in the time strengthening and maintaining your friendships, there will be someone ready to be there for you when you need them.

Imagining a bigger change

What might it mean to not just build up your social ties but to radically reimagine what friendships could mean in your life and also to the outside world?

What if you could commit to a friend as deeply as you would to a romantic partner? That's the idea at the heart of *The Other Significant Others* by Rhaina Cohen. In her book, Cohen explores what it means to center friendship in a world dominated by marriage. In one chapter, she profiles two friends, Lynda and Natasha, who became the first platonic co-parents recognized by the Canadian government. They were able to define their qualifications for parenting by their relationship to a child, not by the relationship between themselves. As Lynda told Cohen, "Romance is wonderful, but I'm not sure it has anything to do with parenting."

What might it mean to co-parent with a friend? Is there a possible route to raise a future child with your sibling or with a few friends?

Another big potential shift may be found in housing. The American dream of homeownership is slipping away for many people. The median price of an existing home in the United States as of November 2023 is $387,600. And if you're in a major city, that price sounds (sadly) too good to be true. The average age of a first-time homeowner in 2022 was thirty-six years old according to the National Association of Realtors. That's a record high.

If you're single, you may have already written off home-ownership entirely. It's frustrating to watch partnered friends with their two incomes being able to afford options beyond your price range. But what would it look like to share the investment in a home with a friend? I've heard multiple friends say how they wish they could live on cheap land surrounded by friends and their families. What if living with friends—perhaps even buying property with friends—could be part of your plan?

The concept of the single-family home is quite new in human history explains Diana Lind in her book *Brave New Home*. Up until World War II, Americans largely had much more communal setups with multigenerational homes and neighborhoods bustling with extended family and friends. Single-family homes can strip away that sense of community and are "unaffordable, unhealthy, and out of step with consumer demand," writes Lind.

Would it make sense for you to buck the current trend? What would it mean to live with roommates by choice, to build a co-living space, or to buy a home with a friend? You don't have to live in a utopian commune, but you can explore what it would mean to share resources with friends in some way.

o o o

If you are someone who longs for a romantic partner, watching others ensconce themselves in their relationships can be lonely. Like you're sitting in a waiting room and everyone else's name is getting called but yours. *What is going on behind that door anyway? Why can't I get invited into that club?*

The longing to jump from your current standing into a seemingly more exclusive community or group is a concept called "the inner ring." It's a phrase used by C. S. Lewis, which I learned via Charles H. Vogl in *The Art of Community*.

Vogl writes that there is some hedonic adaptation at play with inner rings. "Unfortunately, when we do get inside these exclusive rings, we always discover that there's an even more attractive and exclusive ring beyond. This pattern will continue forever unless we break it. This is the trap of the inner ring." To me, coupledom can feel like an inner ring. Instead of trying to gain access to a group that you might not even like, the escape hatch is to "find something we like to do and do it often. Then invite others to join us if they like doing that thing too," explains Vogl. This is, simply, friendship. "As we regularly gather to do this, we'll form a specific kind of relationship that saves us from longing to be elsewhere." Do things that make you happy and friendship will follow. Create your own rings.

ACTIVITY

- List three values you want to be at the center of your community. Set a timer for five minutes and brainstorm as many potential rituals that embody those values as you can.

- Take some social connection inventory. Document a week of social activities, note the quality of the experiences, and evaluate how they made you feel. Which events feel like obligations vs. connective? How can you transform your time with friends into more meaningful moments?

- Reach out to someone who's an acquaintance you admire and invite them for an intentional hangout—maybe an afternoon window shopping, a new museum exhibit, a craft night.

- Start a standing recurring social event for your community. Pick a night and an activity. Commit to hosting it for at least six months.

PRACTICE

- Remember, friendships require tending. To center friendship, you need to show up, check in, and be flexible.

- Don't wait for friendship to happen to you. Make the overture to hang out. The more specific the activity, the better. That way you don't fall into the "we should get lunch soon" trap (reader: they never did meet for that lunch).

- Get in the habit of communicating your needs to friends. Then, be open to being flexible when they tell you theirs.

Epilogue

THERE IS A HAZE THAT CAN SURROUND SOME-
one who's single. A gauzy, all-consuming haze that clouds
your vision. But now when it tells you how to feel about your
singleness, urges you to stress about finding your so-called
other half, you see right through it. As you peel away the
mounds of fuzz, the haze will protest.

*But you need to work harder! Don't you want to be happy?
This means you'll be sad and lonely forever!*

You now know those are empty threats. Recognizing the
shame, stigma, and negative emotions around singleness
means you can separate yourself from them. They were never
you, anyway. Hopefully the tools in this book can help you
see clearly: You are your own soulmate.

And the truth is? There could be lots of romantic relationships—short and long—in your life. Or you could be single
forever, and that would also be terrific! No matter where your
life goes, the commitment you've made to protect your peace
and prioritize your relationship with yourself will ground

and support you. You've done the work that many people shy away from their entire lives—to truly be with themselves. In your new, self-assured way, you can ride the dips and swells of life instead of being crushed if a relationship doesn't work out. Partnerships and romance change or even end. But we always have ourselves. And aren't we great?

Singleness does not mean being on a waitlist to an exclusive party. You have a rich life already, so remember to enjoy it now. I know that if you reach a little deeper into yourself, you won't find emptiness. You'll find confetti. You get to toss it in the air and watch the glittering magic surround you.

Notes

CHAPTER 1

"A fairy-tale expert" Burton, Sarah. "How Fairy Tales Fueled Our Obsession with Weddings." *Huffington Post*. February 13, 2019. https://www. huffpost.com/entry/disney-fairy-tales-fueled-obsession-with-weddings_n_5c5b353be4b08710475a30d9.

"expand their resources and influence" Coontz, Stephanie. 2006. *Marriage, a History: How Love Conquered Marriage*. Penguin Random House, 54.

"plague" Coontz, Stephanie. 2006. *Marriage, a History: How Love Conquered Marriage*. Penguin Random House, 127.

"interdynastic hypogamy" Diel, Lori B. "Till Death Do Us Part: Unconventional Marriages as Aztec Political Strategy." *Ancient Mesoamerica* 18 (2007): 259–272. Accessed September 12, 2023. https://doi.org/10.1017/S0956536107000181.

"King Zimri-lim" Coontz, Stephanie. 2006. *Marriage, a History: How Love Conquered Marriage*. Penguin Random House, 55.

"between humans and Gods as a means to consolidate power" Coontz, Stephanie. 2006. *Marriage, a History: How Love Conquered Marriage*. Penguin Random House, 59–60.

"head and master law" Wikipedia. 2023. "Head and Master Law." Wikimedia Foundation. Last modified July 8, 2023. https://en.wikipedia.org/wiki/Head_and_Master_law.

"Equal Credit Opportunity Act" Issa, Erin E. "Women and Credit Through the Decades: The 1970s." NerdWallet. May 17, 2023. https://www.nerdwallet.com/article/credit-cards/women-credit-decades-70s.

"marital rape" Bennice, Jennifer A., and Patricia A. Resick. "Marital Rape: History, Research, and Practice." *Trauma, Violence & Abuse* 4, no. 3 (2003): 228–246. http://www.jstor.org/stable/26636357.

"sharing food" Cell Press. "What hunter-gatherers can tell us about fundamental human social networks." ScienceDaily. July 21, 2016. www.sciencedaily.com/releases/2016/07/160721142526.htm.

"evidence of polyamory" Johnson, Eric M. "The Case of the Missing Polygamists." *Scientific American*. January 6, 2012. https://blogs.scientificamerican.com/primate-diaries/case-of-the-missing-polygamists/.

"more egalitarian culture" Copland, Simon. "Equality and Polyamory: Why Early Humans Weren't The Flintstones." *The Guardian*. May 19, 2015. https://www.theguardian.com/science/blog/2015/may/19/equality-and-polyamory-why-early-humans-werent-the-flintstones.

"mutual loyalty, duty and protection" Phegley, Jennifer. 2012. *Courtship and Marriage in Victorian England*. ABC-CLIO.

"harmful propaganda disguised as relationship self-help books" Ward, Jane. "The White Supremacist Origins of Modern Marriage Advice." The Conversation. August 27, 2020. https://theconversation.com/the-white-supremacist-origins-of-modern-marriage-advice-144782.

"the median age of an American woman at her first marriage" "Historical Marital Status Tables." Census.gov. United States Census Bureau, November 1, 2022. https://www.census.gov/data/tables/time-series/demo/families/marital.html.

"tax code" Gauff, Tonya M. "Eliminating the Secondary Earner Bias: Lessons from Malaysia, the United Kingdom, and Ireland." *Northwestern Journal of Law & Social Policy* 4, no. 2 (2009). Accessed September 13, 2023. https://scholarlycommons.law.northwestern.edu/njlsp/vol4/iss2/5.

"Stanley Surrey" Gauff, Tonya M. "Eliminating the Secondary Earner Bias: Lessons from Malaysia, the United Kingdom, and Ireland." *Northwestern Journal of Law & Social Policy* 4, no. 2 (2009). Accessed September 13, 2023. https://scholarlycommons.law.northwestern.edu/njlsp/vol4/iss2/5.

"increase in wages for the first time in years" "Income of Families and Persons in the United States: 1950." Census.gov. United States Census Bureau, March 25, 1952. https://www.census.gov/library/publications/1952/demo/p60-009.html.

"easier than ever to be a homemaker" Coontz, Stephanie. 2006. *Marriage, a History: How Love Conquered Marriage*. Penguin Random House, 230–232.

"spent more time with their children than parents of the mid-1960s" Dotti Sani, Giulia M., and Judith Treas. "Educational Gradients in Parents' Child-Care Time Across Countries, 1965–2012." *Journal of Marriage and Family* 78, no. 4 (2016): 1083–1096. Accessed September 13, 2023. https://doi.org/10.1111/jomf.12305.

"it took more than 150 years to establish the love-based, male breadwinner marriage" Coontz, Stephanie. 2006. *Marriage, a History: How Love Conquered Marriage*. Penguin Random House, 247.

"marriage rates do seem to be on the decline" Swanson, Ana. "144 Years of Marriage and Divorce in the United States, in One Chart." *Washington Post*, June 23, 2015. https://www.washingtonpost.com/news/wonk/wp/2015/06/23/144-years-of-marriage-and-divorce-in-the-united-states-in-one-chart/.

"there was a record in the percentage of married couples" United States Census Bureau (September 11, 1961). "1960 Census: Supplementary Reports: Marital Status of the Population of the United States, by States: 1960." Census.gov. Accessed September 13, 2023. https://www.census.gov/library/publications/1961/dec/pc-s1-12.html.

"From 2006 to 2016, the number of never married twenty-five- to twenty-nine-year-olds" Mayol-Garcia, Yeris, Benjamin Gurrentz, and Rose M. Kreider. "Number, Timing, and Duration of Marriages and Divorces: 2016." Census.gov. United States Census Bureau, April 22, 2021. https://www.census.gov/content/dam/Census/library/publications/2021/demo/p70-167.pdf.

"As of 2017, the average age of a woman in Sweden" Ortiz-Ospina, Esteban, and Max Roser. "Marriage and Divorces." Our World in Data, 2020. Accessed September 13, 2023. https://ourworldindata.org/marriages-and-divorces.

"A 2019 Pew Research Center study" Barroso, Amanda. "More than Half of Americans Say Marriage Is Important but Not Essential to Leading a Fulfilling Life." Pew Research Center. February 14, 2020. https://www.pewresearch.org/fact-tank/2020/02/14/more-than-half-of-americans-say-marriage-is-important-but-not-essential-to-leading-a-fulfilling-life/.

"according to Eli Finkel at Northwestern University" Finkel, Eli J., Elaine O. Cheung, Lydia F. Emery, Kathleen L. Carswell, and Grace M. Larson. "The Suffocation Model." *Current Directions in Psychological Science* (2015). Accessed September 13, 2023. https://doi.org/10.1177/0963721415569274.

"amatonormativity" Brake, Elizabeth. 2012. *Minimizing Marriage: Marriage, Morality, and the Law.* Oxford University Press, 88.

"cultural invisibility" Brake, Elizabeth. 2012. *Minimizing Marriage: Marriage, Morality, and the Law.* Oxford University Press, 89.

"Family tends to be understood, for legal and census purposes" Brake, Elizabeth. 2012. *Minimizing Marriage: Marriage, Morality, and the Law.* Oxford University Press, 91.

"family status" Brake, Elizabeth. 2012. *Minimizing Marriage: Marriage, Morality, and the Law.* Oxford University Press.

"biological bribery" Machin, Anna. 2022. *Why We Love: The New Science Behind Our Closest Relationships.* Simon and Schuster, 21.

"re-engage with and celebrate the different types of love" Machin, Anna. "Romantic Love Isn't What It's Cracked up to Be. Here's Why We Don't Need It." *The Guardian*, February 13, 2022. https://www.theguardian.com/lifeandstyle/2022/feb/13/romantic-love-different-ways-to-connect.

"Any hierarchy of importance is a cultural construct" Machin, Anna. "Romantic Love Isn't What It's Cracked up to Be. Here's Why We Don't Need It." *The Guardian*, February 13, 2022. https://www.theguardian.com/lifeandstyle/2022/feb/13/romantic-love-different-ways-to-connect.

CHAPTER 2

"How to Be Single and Happy" Taitz, Jennifer L. 2018. *How to Be Single and Happy: Science-Based Strategies for Keeping Your Sanity While Looking for a Soul Mate.* Penguin Random House.

"happiness set point" Lucas, Richard E., Andrew E. Clark, Yannis Georgellis, and Ed Diener. "Reexamining Adaptation and the Set Point Model of Happiness: Reactions to Changes in Marital Status." *Journal of Personality and Social Psychology* 84, no. 3 (2003): 527–39. Accessed September 8, 2023. https://doi.org/10.1037//0022-3514.84.3.527.

"hedonic treadmill" Wikipedia. 2023. "Hedonic Treadmill." Wikimedia Foundation. Last modified August 23, 2023. https://en.wikipedia.org/wiki/Hedonic_treadmill.

"Singlism" DePaulo, Bella. "Singlism And Matrimania." Bella DePaulo. November 7, 2018. https://www.belladepaulo.com/2018/11/singlism-and-matrimania/.

"perceived singles as less well adjusted and more selfish than their married peers" DePaulo, Bella, and Wendy L. Morris. "Singles in Society and Science." *Psychological Inquiry* 16, no. 2 (2005). Accessed September 8, 2023. https://doi.org/10.1207/s15327965pli162&3_01.

"Studies show that singles are more likely to have broader social groups" Burton-Chellew, Maxwell N., and Robin I. Dunbar. "Romance and Reproduction Are Socially Costly." *Evolutionary Behavioral Sciences* 9, no. 4 (2015): 229–241. Accessed September 4, 2023. https://doi.org/10.1037/ebs0000046.

"meaning they often have *more* friends and are more likely to contact and receive help from extended family than those who are married" Sarkisian, Natalia, and Gerstel, Naomi. "Does Singlehood Isolate or Integrate? Examining the Link Between Marital Status and Ties to Kin, Friends, and Neighbors." *Journal of Social and Personal Relationships* 33, no. 3 (2016): 361–384. https://journals.sagepub.com/doi/full/10.1177/0265407515597564.

"yearning for something you don't have" Kislev, Elyakim. 2019. *Happy Singlehood*. 1st ed. University of California Press. https://www.perlego.com/book/869232/happy-singlehood-the-rising-acceptance-and-celebration-of-solo-living-pdf.

"the more single people want a relationship, the less likely they are to be satisfied with their life" Kislev, Elyakim. "Relationship Desire and Life Satisfaction among Never-married and Divorced Men and Women." *Sexual and Relationship Therapy* (2022). Accessed September 5, 2023. https://doi.org/10.1080/14681994.2022.2099538.

"Core beliefs" "What Are Core Beliefs and How Do They Affect Your Health?" PsychCentral. January 26, 2022. https://psychcentral.com/health/core-beliefs-examples.

"not only is loneliness bad for you" Steptoe, Andrew, Natalie Owen, Sabine R. Kunz-Ebrecht, and Lena Brydon. "Loneliness and Neuroendocrine, Cardiovascular, and Inflammatory Stress Responses in Middle-aged Men and Women." *Psychoneuroendocrinology* 29, no. 5 (2003): 593–611. Accessed September 5, 2023. https://doi.org/10.1016/S0306-4530(03)00086-6.

"loneliness is worse than smoking 15 cigarettes a day" Murthy, Vivek H. "Our Epidemic of Loneliness and Isolation: The U.S. Surgeon General's Advisory on the Healing Effects of Social Connection and Community." HHS.gov. U.S. Department of Health and Human Services, May 3, 2023. https://www.hhs.gov/sites/default/files/surgeon-general-social-connection-advisory.pdf.

"social isolation is associated with higher risks of anxiety, depression, heart disease, and dementia" "Loneliness and Social Isolation Linked to Serious Health Conditions." Centers for Disease Control and Prevention. April 29, 2021. https://doi.org/10.17226/25663.

"2023 US Surgeon General's advisory" Murthy, Vivek H. "Our Epidemic of Loneliness and Isolation: The U.S. Surgeon General's Advisory on the Healing Effects of Social Connection and Community." HHS.gov. U.S. Department of Health and Human Services, May 3, 2023. https://www.hhs.gov/sites/default/files/surgeon-general-social-connection-advisory.pdf.

"Loneliness means being dissatisfied with being alone." Cacioppo, John T., Louise Hawley, and Gary Berntson. "The Anatomy of Loneliness." *Current Directions in Psychological Science* 12, no. 3 (2003): 71–74. Accessed September 5, 2023. https://doi.org/10.1111/1467-8721.01232.

"state of painful loneliness" "The Lethality of Loneliness." TEDx Talks. YouTube. September 9, 2013. https://www.youtube.com/watch?v=_0hxl03JoA0.

"loneliness is a biological signal akin to hunger or thirst" Cacioppo, John T., and William Patrick. 2008. *Loneliness: Human Nature and the Need for Social Connection.* W.W. Norton & Company, 18.

"loneliness is a warning signal" Cacioppo, John T., and William Patrick. 2008. *Loneliness: Human Nature and the Need for Social Connection.* W.W. Norton & Company, 59.

"Connection thrives on quality over quantity." The Lethality of Loneliness." TEDx Talks. YouTube. September 9, 2013. https://www.youtube.com/watch?v=_0hxl03JoA0.

"Solitude is a neutral to positive state of being free of the demands of others" Rodriguez, Micaela, Benjamin W. Bellet, and Richard J. McNally. "Reframing Time Spent Alone: Reappraisal Buffers the Emotional Effects of Isolation." *Cognitive Therapy and Research* 44 (2020): 1052–1067. Accessed September 5, 2023. https://doi.org/10.1007/s10608-020-10128-x.

"fifteen minutes of solitude can help you regulate your emotions" Nguyen, Thuy-vy T., Richard M. Ryan, and Edward L. Deci. "Solitude as an Approach to Affective Self-Regulation." *Personality and Social Psychology Bulletin* 44, no. 1 (2017): 92–106. Accessed September 5, 2023. https://doi.org/10.1177/0146167217733073.

"shift negative beliefs about alone time" Rodriguez, Micaela, Benjamin W. Bellet, and Richard J. McNally. "Reframing Time Spent Alone: Reappraisal Buffers the Emotional Effects of Isolation." *Cognitive Therapy and Research* 44 (2020): 1052–1067. Accessed September 5, 2023. https://doi.org/10.1007/s10608-020-10128-x.

"people are more likely to prefer to go to a movie with a friend on a Saturday night" Kaplan, Melanie D. "The Value of Going Alone." McDonough School of Business. June 28, 2017. https://msb.georgetown.edu/news-story/value-going-alone/.

"people tend to *underestimate* how much they will enjoy a solo activity" Ratner, Rebecca K., and Rebecca W. Hamilton. "Inhibited from Bowling Alone." *Journal of Consumer Research* 42, no. 2 (2015): 266–283. Accessed May 28, 2015. https://doi.org/10.1093/jcr/ucv012.

"boredom . . . we are looking to engage in an activity without knowing what to latch on to" Danckert, James, and John Eastwood. "Why Does Boredom Exist?" *Psychology Today.* June 1, 2020. https://www. psychologytoday.com/us/blog/the-engaged-mind/202006/why-does-boredom-exist.

"help fuel creative thinking" Bowker, Julie C., Miriam T. Stotsky, and Rebecca G. Etkin. "How BIS/BAS and Psycho-behavioral Variables Distinguish between Social Withdrawal Subtypes during Emerging Adulthood." Personality and Individual Differences 119, no. 1 (2017): 283–288. Accessed September 5, 2023. https://doi.org/10.1016/ j.paid.2017.07.043.

"morning pages . . . artist date" Cameron, Julia. 2016. *The Artist's Way: A Spiritual Path to Higher Creativity.* TarcherPerigee.

"people tend to enjoy a solo visit to an art gallery as much as if they went with a friend" "The Upside of All of This Alone Time." Robert H. Smith School of Business, University of Maryland. May 29, 2020. https://www.rhsmith.umd.edu/research/upside-all-alone-time.

"internal and subjective sense of connection" Seppala, Emma. "Connectedness & Health: The Science of Social Connection." The Center for Compassion and Altruism Research and Education. May 8, 2014. https://ccare.stanford.edu/uncategorized/connectedness-health-the-science-of-social-connection-infographic/.

"research that suggests doing good deeds for others is more effective at raising our happiness levels than doing something for ourselves" Titova, Milla, and Kennon Sheldon. "Happiness Comes from Trying to Make Others Feel Good, Rather Than Oneself." *The Journal of Positive Psychology* 17, no. 1 (2019): 1–15. Accessed September 5, 2023. https:// doi.org/10.1080/17439760.2021.1897867.

"Loving-kindness meditation" "A Meditation on Lovingkindness." Jack Kornfield. October 2, 2014. https://jackkornfield.com/meditation-lovingkindness/.

"loving-kindness meditation has been found to increase positive emotions like joy, awe, and hope" Fredrickson, Barbara L., Michael A. Cohn, Kimberly A. Coffey, Jolynn Pek, and Sandra M. Finkel. "Open Hearts Build Lives: Positive Emotions, Induced through Loving-kindness Meditation, Build Consequential Personal Resources." *Journal of Personality and Social Psychology* 95, no. 5 (2005): 1045–1062. Accessed September 5, 2023. https://doi.org/10.1037/a0013262.

"UC Davis gratitude researcher Robert Emmons found this kind of regular practice" Emmons, Robert A., and Michael E. McCullough. "Counting Blessings versus Burdens: An Experimental Investigation of Gratitude and Subjective Well-being in Daily Life." *Journal of Personality and Social Psychology* 84, no. 2 (2003): 377–389. Accessed September 5, 2023. https://doi.org/10.1037//0022-3514.84.2.377.

"Emmons also found that the folks who kept a gratitude journal" Emmons, Robert. "Gratitude and Well-Being." Gratitude Works. Accessed September 5, 2023. https://emmons.faculty.ucdavis.edu/gratitude-and-well-being/.

CHAPTER 3

"Repetitive negative thinking can be a common symptom of anxiety and depression" Kertz, Sarah J., Jennifer Koran, Kimberly T. Stevens, and Thröstur Björgvinsson. "Repetitive Negative Thinking Predicts Depression and Anxiety Symptom Improvement during Brief Cognitive Behavioral Therapy." *Behavior Research and Therapy* (2015). Accessed August 31, 2023. https://pubmed.ncbi.nlm.nih.gov/25812825/.

"thinking about the past can lead to negative moods—even if the content of the thoughts are positive" Ruby, Florence J., Jonathan Smallwood, Haakon Engen, and Tania Singer. "How Self-Generated

Thought Shapes Mood—The Relation between Mind-Wandering and Mood Depends on the Socio-Temporal Content of Thoughts." *PLoS One* (2013). Accessed August 31, 2023. https://doi.org/10.1371/journal. pone.0077554.

"regulates thoughts, emotions, and action" Arnsten, Amy F. "Stress Signalling Pathways That Impair Prefrontal Cortex Structure and Function." *Nature Reviews Neuroscience* 10 (2009): 410–422. Accessed August 31, 2023. https://doi.org/10.1038/nrn2648.

"overthinking things actually consumes your executive functions" Kross, Ethan. 2021. *Chatter: The Voice in Our Head, Why It Matters, and How to Harness It.* Penguin Random House.

"fear + uncertainty = anxiety" Brewer, Judson A. 2021. *Unwinding Anxiety: New Science Shows How to Break the Cycles of Worry and Fear to Heal Your Mind.* Penguin Random House, 19.

"1. Trigger 2. Behavior 3. Result" Brewer, Judson A. 2021. *Unwinding Anxiety: New Science Shows How to Break the Cycles of Worry and Fear to Health Your Mind.* Penguin Random House, 32.

"chronic state of activated stress" Szabo, Yvette Z., Christina M. Burns, and Crystal Lantrip. "Understanding Associations between Rumination and Inflammation: A Scoping Review." *Neuroscience & Biobehavioral Reviews* (2021). Accessed August 31, 2023. https://doi.org/10.1016/j.neubiorev.2022.104523.

"contrary evidence about their political beliefs" Kaplan, Jonas T., Sarah I. Gimbel, and Sam Harris. "Neural Correlates of Maintaining One's Political Beliefs in the Face of Counterevidence." *Scientific Reports* 6, no. 1 (2016): 1–11. Accessed January 13, 2024. https://doi.org/10.1038/srep39589.

"dwelling on something repeatedly" "Rumination: A Cycle of Negative Thinking." American Psychiatric Association. March 5, 2020. https://www.psychiatry.org/News-room/APA-Blogs/Rumination-A-Cycle-of-Negative-Thinking.

"example in his book: You're having car trouble" Watkins, Edward R. 2015. *Rumination-Focused Cognitive-Behavioral Therapy for Depression.* The Guilford Press.

"A study by psychologists Sonja Lyubomirsky and Susan Nolen-Hoeksema" Lyubomirsky, Sonja, and Susan Nolen-Hoeksema. "Self-perpetuating Properties of Dysphoric Rumination." *Journal of Personality and Social Psychology* (1993). Accessed August 31, 2023. https://doi.org/10.1037//0022-3514.65.2.339.

"participants venting frustrations via online communication were more likely to have their negative feelings linger" Kross, Ethan, David Lee, Ariana Orvell, Julia Briskin, Taylor Shrapnell, Susan A. Gelman, Ozlem Ayduk, and Oscar Ybarra. "When Chatting About Negative Experiences Helps—and When It Hurts: Distinguishing Adaptive Versus Maladaptive Social Support in Computer-Mediated Communication." *Emotion* 20, no. 3 (2017). https://doi.org/10.1037/emo0000555.

"prime us to respond with aggressive thoughts" Bushman, Brad J. "Does Venting Anger Feed or Extinguish the Flame? Catharsis, Rumination, Distraction, Anger and Aggressive Responding." *Personality and Social Psychology Bulletin* 28, no. 6 (2003): 724–731. Accessed September 1, 2023.

"perceived vastness" Reese, Hope. "How a Bit of Awe Can Improve Your Health." *New York Times*, January 3, 2023. https://www.nytimes.com/2023/01/03/well/live/awe-wonder-dacher-keltner.html.

"being in the presence of something larger than ourselves helps quiet our nervous system" Chirico, Alice, Pietro Cipresso, David B. Yaden, Federica Biassoni, Giuseppe Riva, and Andrea Gaggioli. "Effectiveness of Immersive Videos in Inducing Awe: An Experimental Study." *Scientific Reports* (2017). Accessed September 1, 2023. https://doi.org/10.1038/s41598-017-01242-0.

"tree-lined street" Kuo, Ming. "How Might Contact with Nature Promote Human Health? Promising Mechanisms and a Possible Central Pathway." *Frontiers in Psychology* 6, no. 1093 (2015). Accessed September 1, 2023. https://doi.org/ 10.3389/fpsyg.2015.01093.

"inspiring speeches or writing" Thomson, Andrew L., and Jason T. Siegel. "Elevation: A Review of Scholarship on a Moral and Other-praising Emotion." *The Journal of Positive Psychology* 12, no. 6 (2016): 628–638. Accessed September 1, 2023. https://doi.org/10.1080/17439760.2016.1269184.

"eight minutes" Nolen-Hoeksema, Susan, and Jannay Morrow. "Effects of Rumination and Distraction on Naturally Occurring Depressed Mood." *Cognition and Emotion* 7, no. 6 (1993): 561–570. Accessed September 1, 2023. https://doi.org/10.1080/02699939308409206.

"comparison trap" Lyubomirsky, Sonja, and Lee Ross. "Hedonic Consequences of Social Comparison: A Contrast of Happy and Unhappy People." *Journal of Personality and Social Psychology* 73, no. 6 (1997): 1141–1157. Accessed September 1, 2023. https://doi.org/10.1037/0022-3514.73.6.1141.

"temporal distancing" Kross, Ethan. 2021. *Chatter: The Voice in Our Head, Why It Matters, and How to Harness It.* Penguin Random House.

"imagining the color, texture, and temperature of your negative thoughts" Bonior, Andrea. 2020. *Detox Your Thoughts: Quit Negative Self-Talk for Good and Discover the Life You've Always Wanted.* Chronicle Books, 36.

"depression-prone college students" Pennebaker, James W., Eva-Maria Gortner, and Stephanie S. Rude. "Benefits of Expressive Writing in Lowering Rumination and Depressive Symptom." *Behavior Therapy* 37, no. 3 (2006): 292–303. Accessed September 4, 2023. https://doi.org/10.1016/j.beth.2006.01.004.

"better accept emotions" Ruini, Chiara, and Cristina C. Mortara. "Writing Technique Across Psychotherapies—From Traditional Expressive Writing to New Positive Psychology Interventions: A Narrative Review." *Journal of Contemporary Psychotherapy* 52 (2022): 23–34.

Accessed September 4, 2023. https://doi.org/10.1007/s10879-021-09520-9.

"reward-based learning" Brewer, Judson A. 2021. *Unwinding Anxiety: New Science Shows How to Break the Cycles of Worry and Fear to Heal Your Mind*. Penguin Random House, 30.

"bigger, better offer" Brewer, Judson A. 2021. *Unwinding Anxiety: New Science Shows How to Break the Cycles of Worry and Fear to Heal Your Mind*. Penguin Random House, 164.

"Brewer found mindful states of curiosity" Brewer, Judson. "Mindfulness Training for Addictions: Has Neuroscience Revealed a Brain Hack by Which Awareness Subverts the Addictive Process?" *Current Opinion in Psychology* 28 (2019): 198–203. Accessed September 4, 2023. https://doi.org/10.1016/j.copsyc.2019.01.014.

CHAPTER 4

"obsessive passion" Vallerand, Robert J. "The Role of Passion in Sustainable Psychological Well-being." *Psychology of Well-Being: Theory, Research and Practice* 2, no. 1 (2012): 1–21. Accessed September 8, 2023. https://doi.org/10.1186/2211-1522-2-1.

"attached to a plan" Fodor, Eugene M., and David P. Wick. "Need for Power and Affective Response to Negative Audience Reaction to an Extemporaneous Speech." *Journal of Research in Personality* 43, no. 5 (2009): 721–726. Accessed September 8, 2023. https://doi.org/10.1016/j.jrp.2009.06.007.

"practicing acceptance" "Radical Acceptance." DBT-RU: DBT Skills from Experts. December 8, 2020. https://youtu.be/vwNnG7mIu1E.

"A. Accumulating positives . . . B. Building mastery . . . C. Coping ahead" Linehan, Marsha M. 2014. *DBT Skills Training Manual*. 2nd ed. Guilford Press, 382.

"I like to smell good" Brown, A. M. 2019. *Pleasure Activism: The Politics of Feeling Good*. AK Press, 6.

"pleasure framework: sensualism" Leboeuf, Céline. "Walking in Simone de Beauvoir's Footsteps." *Medium*. September 28, 2019. https://medium.com/the-philosophers-stone/walking-in-simone-de-beauvoirs-footsteps-db6a5c08b550.

"different way of living the body" Leboeuf, Céline. "Simone de Beauvoir's Feminist Art of Living." *The Journal of Speculative Philosophy* 33, no. 3 (2019): 448–460. https://doi.org/10.5325/jspecphil.33.3.0448.

"women are still doing the majority of the housework" Fry, Richard, Carolina Aragão, Kiley Hurst, and Kim Parker. "In a Growing Share of U.S. Marriages, Husbands and Wives Earn About the Same." Pew Research. April 13, 2023. https://www.pewresearch.org/social-trends/2023/04/13/in-a-growing-share-of-u-s-marriages-husbands-and-wives-earn-about-the-same/.

"median wealth of married people under age thirty-five" Sullivan, Briana, Donald Hays, and Neil Bennett. "The Wealth of Households: 2021." Census.gov. US Census. Accessed January 21, 2024. https://www.census.gov/content/dam/Census/library/publications/2023/demo/p70br-183.pdf.

"they still make only 92.1 percent of what single men make" Ceron, Ella. "The Pay Gap for Single Women Is Getting Worse." *Time*, March 8, 2023. https://time.com/6260969/gender-pay-gap-single-women/.

"one in three" Egan, John, and Kelly A. Smith. "Study: Vast Majority of Single Americans Feel Burden of 'Singles Tax'." *Forbes*, May 25, 2023. https://www.forbes.com/advisor/personal-finance/survey-singles-tax/.

"hobbies . . . better mood, lower heart rate, and less stress" Zawadzki, Matthew J., Joshua M. Smyth, and Heather J. Costigan. "Real-Time Associations Between Engaging in Leisure and Daily Health and Well-Being." *The Annuals of Behavioral Medicine* 49, no. 4 (2015): 605–615. Accessed September 8, 2023. https://doi.org/10.1007/s12160-015-9694-3.

"Pets foster a sense of belonging and connection" Corliss, Julie. "The Heartfelt Benefits of Pet Ownership." Harvard Health Publishing, Harvard Medical School. December 12, 2022. https://www.health.harvard.edu/heart-health/the-heartfelt-benefits-of-pet-ownership.

"Researchers have found that cortisol levels drop when people spend time with dogs for even just five minutes" Godoy, Maria. "Petting Other People's Dogs, Even Briefly, Can Boost Your Health." NPR. August 3, 2023. https://www.npr.org/sections/health-shots/2023/08/03/1190728554/dog-pet-mental-health-benefits.

"Dr. Pooja Lakshmin writes" Lakshmin, Pooja. 2023. *Real Self-Care: A Transformative Program for Redefining Wellness (Crystals, Cleanses, and Bubble Baths Not Included)*. Penguin Life, 166.

"goals are the things that you do, values are the way you do them" Lakshmin, Pooja. 2023. *Real Self-Care: A Transformative Program for Redefining Wellness (Crystals, Cleanses, and Bubble Baths Not Included)*. Penguin Life, 165.

"how values work" Brown, Duane, and R. K. Crace. "Values in Life Role Choices and Outcomes: A Conceptual Model." *The Career Development Quarterly* 44, no. 3 (1996): 211–223. Accessed January 10, 2024. https://doi.org/10.1002/j.2161-0045.1996.tb00252.x.

"flourishing" Ambler, Virginia M., Robert Kelly Crace, and Jodi Fisler. "Nurturing Genius: Positive Psychology as a Framework for Organization and Practice." *About Campus* 19, no. 6 (2015). https://www.researchgate.net/publication/272524858_Nurturing_Genius_Positive_Psychology_as_a_Framework_for_Organization_and_Practice.

"wise mind" Elices, Matilde, Joaquim Soler, Albert Feliu-Soler, Cristina Carmona, Thais Tiana, Juan C. Pascual, Azucena García-Palacios, and Enric Álvarez. "Combining Emotion Regulation and Mindfulness Skills for Preventing Depression Relapse: A Randomized-controlled Study." *Borderline Personality Disorder and Emotion Dysregulation*

4, (2017). Accessed September 28, 2023. https://doi.org/10.1186/s40479-017-0064-6.

CHAPTER 5

"the mind as divided up into different regions" Barrett, Lisa F. "The Theory of Constructed Emotion: An Active Inference Account of Interoception and Categorization." *Social Cognitive and Affective Neuroscience* 12, no. 1 (2017): 1–23. Accessed September 5, 2023. https://doi.org/10.1093/scan/nsw154.

"found that no singular brain region was responsible for any specific emotion" Barrett, Lisa F. "What Emotions Are (and Aren't)." *New York Times*, July 31, 2015. https://www.nytimes.com/2015/08/02/opinion/sunday/what-emotions-are-and-arent.html.

"pleasantness and unpleasantness and another level" Spiegel, Alix. "Emotions." *Invisibilia*. NPR, June 1, 2017. https://www.npr.org/2017/06/01/530928414/emotions-part-one.

"emotional regulation" Wikipedia. 2023. "Emotional Self-regulation." Wikimedia Foundation. Last modified August 12, 2023. https://en.wikipedia.org/wiki/Emotional_self-regulation.

"emotional dysregulation" "Emotional Dysregulation." Cleveland Clinic. June 9, 2023. https://my.clevelandclinic.org/health/symptoms/25065-emotional-dysregulation.

"managing anxiety, depression, and stress" Parsons, Dave, Peter Gardner, Sharon Parry, and Sharon Smart. "Mindfulness-Based Approaches for Managing Stress, Anxiety and Depression for Health Students in Tertiary Education: A Scoping Review." *Mindfulness* 13, no. 1 (2022): 1–16. Accessed September 6, 2023. https://doi.org/10.1007/s12671-021-01740-3.

"sleep better" Rusch, Heather L., Michael Rosario, Lisa M. Levison, Anlys Olivera, Whitney S. Livingston, Tianxia Wu, and Jessica M. Gill. "The Effect of Mindfulness Meditation on Sleep Quality: A Systematic

Review and Meta-analysis of Randomized Controlled Trials." *Annals of the New York Academy of Sciences* 1445, no. 1 (2019): 5. Accessed September 6, 2023. https://doi.org/10.1111/nyas.13996.

"chronic illnesses" Zeidan, Fadel, and David Vago. "Mindfulness Meditation–Based Pain Relief: A Mechanistic Account." *Annals of the New York Academy of Sciences* 1373, no. 1 (2016): 114. Accessed September 6, 2023. https://doi.org/10.1111/nyas.13153.

"mindfulness is paying attention to the present moment on purpose and without judgment" Kabat-Zinn, Jon. 2012. *Mindfulness for Beginners: Reclaiming the Present Moment—And Your Life.* Sounds True.

"Cold can help activate the parasympathetic nervous system" Mäkinen, Tiina M., Matti Mäntysaari, Tiina Pääkkönen, Jari Jokelainen, Lawrence A. Palinkas, Juhani Hassi, Juhani Leppäluoto, Kari Tahvanainen, and Hannu Rintamäki. "Autonomic Nervous Function during Whole-body Cold Exposure before and after Cold Acclimation." *Aviation, Space, and Environmental Medicine* 79, no. 9 (2008): 875–882. Accessed September 6, 2023. https://doi.org/10.3357/asem.2235.2008.

"2018 study showed cold exposure can help slow your heart rate" Jungmann, Manuela, Shervin Vencatachellum, Dimitri V. Ryckeghem, and Claus Vögele. "Effects of Cold Stimulation on Cardiac-Vagal Activation in Healthy Participants: Randomized Controlled Trial." *JMIR Formative Research* 2, no. 2 (2018). Accessed September 6, 2023. https://doi.org/10.2196/10257.

"deep breathing" Jerath, Ravinder, Molly W. Crawford, Vernon A. Barnes, and Kyler Harden. "Self-Regulation of Breathing as a Primary Treatment for Anxiety." *Applied Psychophysiology and Biofeedback* 40 (2015): 107–115. Accessed September 6, 2023. https://doi.org/10.1007/s10484-015-9279-8.

"activating that parasympathetic nervous" Komori, Teruhisa. "The Relaxation Effect of Prolonged Expiratory Breathing." *Mental Illness*

10, no. 1 (2018). Accessed September 6, 2023. https://doi.org/10.4081/mi.2018.7669.

"lojong teaching" Chodron, Pema. 2021. *Start Where You Are: A Guide to Compassionate Living.* Shambhala, 88.

"alcohol impacts serotonin levels, which can often worsen anxiety" "Anxiety and Alcohol: Does Drinking Worsen Symptoms?" Cleveland Clinic. September 16, 2022. https://health.clevelandclinic.org/emotional-hangover-why-alcohol-can-give-you-anxiety/.

"short bursts of movement can impact anxiety levels." Basso, Julia C., and Wendy A. Suzuki. "The Effects of Acute Exercise on Mood, Cognition, Neurophysiology, and Neurochemical Pathways: A Review." *Brain Plasticity* 2, no. 2 (2017): 127–152. Accessed September 6, 2023. https://doi.org/10.3233/BPL-160040.

"anger iceberg" Regan, Sarah, and Nicole Beurkens. "How to Use the Anger Iceberg to Work Through Conflict & Emotions." MBG Mindfulness. June 28, 2020. https://www.mindbodygreen.com/articles/the-anger-iceberg-and-how-to-work-with-it-effectively.

"near enemy" Kornfield, Jack. *Bringing Home the Dharma: Awakening Right Where You Are.* Shambhala, 2012.

CHAPTER 6

"good relationships keep us happier and healthier" Waldinger, Robert, and Marc Schulz. 2022. *The Good Life: Lessons from the World's Longest Scientific Study of Happiness.* Simon and Schuster, 10.

"positive friendships, family relationships, casual acquaintances" Dickinson, Kevin. "Want to Live a Happy Life? Focus on Your Relationships." Big Think. January 13, 2023. https://bigthink.com/the-learning-curve/want-to-live-a-happy-life-focus-on-your-relationships/.

"Swedish men" Orth-Gomér, Kristina, Annika Rosengren, and Lars Wilhelmsen. "Lack of Social Support and Incidence of Coronary Heart Disease in Middle-aged Swedish Men." *Psychosomatic Medicine* 55, no. 1 (1994): 37–42. Accessed September 8, 2023. https://journals.lww. com/psychosomaticmedicine/Citation/1993/01000/Lack_of_social_ support_and_incidence_of_coronary.7.aspx.

"older age had a bigger impact on happiness than family" Chopik, Willam J. "Associations among Relational Values, Support, Health, and Well-being across the Adult Lifespan." *Personal Relationships* 24, no. 2 (2017): 408–422. Accessed September 8, 2023.

"Singles tend to have more social connections than married people" McConchie, James. "One Key to Being Happy When You're Single." *Greater Good Magazine.* University of California, Berkeley, November 4, 2019. https://greatergood.berkeley.edu/article/item/one_key_to_ being_happy_when_youre_single. See also Sarkisian, Natalia, and Naomi Gerstel. "Does Singlehood Isolate or Integrate? Examining the Link between Marital Status and Ties to Kin, Friends, and Neighbors." *Journal of Social and Personal Relationships* (2015). Accessed September 8, 2023. https://doi.org/10.1177/0265407515597564.

"singles can also surpass married couples in happiness if they are proactive about their friendships" McConchie, James. "One Key to Being Happy When You're Single." *Greater Good Magazine.* University of California, Berkeley, November 4, 2019. https://greatergood.berkeley. edu/article/item/one_key_to_being_happy_when_youre_single

"weak ties" Granovetter, Mark S. "The Strength of Weak Ties." *American Journal of Sociology* 78, no. 6 (1973): 1360–1380. http://www.jstor.org/ stable/2776392.

"low-stakes kind of connection" Sandstrom, Gillian M., and Elizabeth W. Dunn. "Social Interactions and Well-Being." *Personality and Social Psychology Bulletin* (2014). Accessed September 8, 2023. https://doi. org/10.1177/0146167214529799.

"communally oriented" Le, Bonnie M., Emily A. Impett, Aleksandr Kogan, Gergory D. Webster, and Cecilia Cheng. "The Personal and Interpersonal Rewards of Communal Orientation." *Journal of*

Social and Personal Relationships 30, no. 6 (2012): 694–710. Accessed September 8, 2023. https://doi.org/10.1177/0265407512466227.

"platonic love" Franco, Marisa G. 2022. *Platonic: How the Science of Attachment Can Help You Make—and Keep—Friends*. G.P Putnam's Sons.

"matching hypothesis" Jia, Tao, Robert F. Spivey, Boleslaw Szymanski, and Gyorgy Korniss. "An Analysis of the Matching Hypothesis in Networks." *PLoS ONE* 10, no. 6 (2015). Accessed September 8, 2023. https://doi.org/10.1371/journal.pone.0129804.

"social fitness" Waldinger, Robert, and Marc Schulz. 2022. *The Good Life: Lessons from the World's Longest Scientific Study of Happiness*. Simon and Schuster, 25.

"crisis of belonging" Vogl, Charles H. 2016. *The Art of Community: Seven Principles for Belonging*. Berrett-Koehler, 46.

"more structured events" Parker, Priya. 2018. *The Art of Gathering: How We Meet and Why It Matters*. Riverhead Books, 26.

"Hospitality is a mindset" Kentgen, Lisa. 2021. *The Practice of Belonging: Six Lessons from Vibrant Communities to Combat Loneliness, Foster Diversity, and Cultivate Caring Relationships*. North Atlantic Books, 149.

"curiosity is a way to acknowledge people" Dickinson, Kevin. "Want to Live a Happy Life? Focus on Your Relationships." *Big Think*. January 13, 2023. https://bigthink.com/the-learning-curve/want-to-live-a-happy-life-focus-on-your-relationships/.

"space in our schedules and lives for spontaneous invitations and lingering conversations" Kentgen, Lisa. 2021. *The Practice of Belonging: Six Lessons from Vibrant Communities to Combat Loneliness, Foster Diversity, and Cultivate Caring Relationships*. North Atlantic Books, 149.

"shine theory" Sow, Aminatou, and Ann Friedman. 2020. *Big Friendship: How We Keep Each Other Close*. Simon & Schuster, 72. See also

Sow, Aminatou, and Ann Friedman. "Shine Theory." https://www.shinetheory.com/.

"People feel good when they can help" DeWitte, Melissa. "Asking for Help Is Hard, but People Want to Help More than We Realize, Stanford Scholar Says." *Stanford News*. Stanford University, September 8, 2022. https://news.stanford.edu/2022/09/08/asking-help-hard-people-want-help-realize/.

"celebrating with loved ones" Brick, Danielle J., Kelley G. Wight, James R. Bettman, Tanya L. Chartrand, and Gavan J. Fitzsimons. "Celebrate Good Times: How Celebrations Increase Perceived Social Support." *Journal of Public Policy & Marketing* (2023). Accessed September 8, 2023. https://doi.org/10.1177/07439156221145696.

"friendships need three main ingredients" Sow, Aminatou, and Ann Friedman. 2020. *Big Friendship: How We Keep Each Other Close*. Simon & Schuster

"reciprocity theory" Falk, Armin, and Urs Fischbacher. "A Theory of Reciprocity." *Games and Economic Behavior* 54, no. 2 (2006): 293–315. Accessed September 8, 2023. https://doi.org/10.1016/j.geb.2005.03.001.

"Romance is wonderful, but I'm not sure it has anything to do with parenting" Cohen, Rhaina. 2024. *The Other Significant Others*. St. Martin's Publishing Group.

"median price of an existing home in the United States" McMillin, David, and Michele Petry. "Median Home Prices in Every State." Bankrate. January 3, 2024. https://www.bankrate.com/real-estate/median-home-price/.

"average age of a first-time homeowner in 2022" "NAR Finds Share of First-Time Home Buyers Smaller, Older Than Ever Before." National Association of Realtors. November 3, 2022. https://www.nar.realtor/newsroom/nar-finds-share-of-first-time-home-buyers-smaller-older-than-ever-before.

"single-family home" Lind, Diana. 2020. *Brave New Home: Our Future in Smarter, Simpler, Happier Housing.* Bold Type Books.

"inner ring" Vogl, Charles H. 2016. *The Art of Community: Seven Principles for Belonging.* Berrett-Koehler.

Acknowledgments

THANK YOU TO LA JOHNSON, my collaborator, who encouraged me every step of the way. This book exists because of you. Thank you for your art, collaboration, and friendship. To Allison Alder, Pamela Geismar, and Dena Rayess at Chronicle Books for believing in this book and helping us shape it. To my agent, Gillian MacKenize, for being my advocate. To Emily Krieger for fact-checking with rigor and humor.

My friends and early readers, Caitlin Dickerson, Jolie Myers, and Thalia Bardell: Thank you for your time, edits, and guidance. And to all the other friends who supported me in this process: Nicolas Coburn, MJ Halberstadt, Sam Sanders, Jinae West, Becky Sullivan, Connor Donevan, Chris Benderev, Dave Blanchard, Bobby Sherwood, Daniel Reis, Alecia Eberhardt-Smith, Julianna Snapp, Kat Lonsdorf, Ali Underwood, Suzanna Bobadilla, Elissa Nadworny, Lauren Graves, Becky Paris, Colleen McClintock, Brent Baughman, Acacia Squires, Yonatan Gebeyehu, Melaura Homan-Smith,

Sherri Borman, David Mendler, Claire Buetow, Deena Guirguis, Alex Toporek, and Jillian Martucci.

Thank you to my family—in particular, my mother, Cynthia, and my aunt Karen. Thank you to my aunt Laura. To the people I wish were still here: my father, James Keane, his brother, and my uncle Marty Keane, Nonnie, and Papa. Thank you all for building me up, raising me right, and loving me every step of the way. To Paul. Thank you for your endless support and accepting me for exactly who I am.

Thank you to my NPR colleagues—Beth Donovan and the *Life Kit* team: Marielle Segarra, Clare Marie Schneider, Audrey Nguyen, Sylvie Douglis, Andee Tagle, Malaka Gharib, Beck Harlan. My work on NPR's *Life Kit* changes my life time and time again. Thank you for your wisdom, lessons, and support.

Thank you to DC Writers Salon and Ali Cherry for their support and a space to write this book. Thank you also to Elise Hu, Rhaina Cohen, Marisa Franco, and all the other writers in my life who gave me advice and encouragement.

To every ex-boyfriend, ex-situationship, ex-crush: Thank you for not working out. I am better off without all of you.

—*Meghan Keane*

THANK YOU TO MEGHAN, the smartest woman I know, who made writing a book look so easy. Thank you for writing this honest book and believing in the combined power of art and words. I'm ever grateful for your friendship and collaboration.

To Gillian, the wisest agent and kindest human in this business. You know a good idea when you see one, and you knew this project would be something big.

To the Chronicle Prism team who took a big chance on us. Allison, thank you for being the glue to this book and getting the big picture; Pamela and the design team, you patiently guided me through this scary new process and I am so happy with the finished product; to the marketing and publicity team for sending the book around to anyone and everyone and making us look amazing; and to the larger Chronicle family, especially Dena, for jiving with our initial pitch and getting to the finish line.

To my NPR colleagues: Steve, thank you for introducing me to Gillian! You are the best brainstorming partner, and I value our friendship; Nicole and Beth, for loving comics and knowing there is a place for them at news organizations; Elissa, I cherish your encouragement, your creativity, and the way you always know how to find the best light; and Malaka, for inspiring me to make more comics, and for advising on how not to get screwed over.

For Michael, my partner of many years, and now husband and father of our children—I still see you as my best friend, above all else. And to my son Jasper—I promise I will never feed you lies inflating the importance of partnering and marriage. I love you two with all my heart.

Thank you to my huge family and many dear friends—especially those of you who have shared your experiences being single—for cheering me on through this process. I love you all, your support means the world to me.

Lastly, thank you to the recently divorced woman in publishing who emailed me suggesting that the NPR comic Meghan and I made together based on Meghan's *Life Kit* episode about being single should be a book. You were right! Thank you for being the spark for this whole thing.

—*LA Johnson*

About the Author and Artist

MEGHAN KEANE is the founder and supervising editor for NPR's *Life Kit*, a podcast and radio show that brings listeners advice and actionable information about personal finances, health, parenting, relationships, and more. Prior to founding *Life Kit*, Keane was a producer for NPR's award-winning podcast *Invisibilia* and a founding producer of NPR's *TED Radio Hour*, one of NPR's top podcasts since its debut. She currently lives with her mini dachshund, Margo, in Washington, DC.

LA JOHNSON is an art director and comics journalist at NPR, as well as an illustrator, an artist, and a mom. She regularly publishes comics on NPR.org that range from how-tos to investigative journalism. She is a two-time winner of the Edward R. Murrow Excellence in Innovation award as part of NPR's education team; a part of the podcast *Code Switch*, No. 1 on Apple; and a member of NPR's how-to podcast *Life Kit*. LA and her family live in Washington, DC.